THE TREADMILL OF CRIME

Drawing on the work of Allan Schnaiberg, this book returns political economy to green criminology and examines how the expansion of capitalism shapes environmental law, crime and justice. The book is organized around crimes of ecological withdrawals and ecological additions.

The Treadmill of Crime is written by acclaimed experts on the subject of green criminology and examines issues such as crime in the energy sector as well as the release of toxic waste into the environment and its impact on ecosystems. This book also sets a new research agenda by highlighting problems of ecological disorganization for animal abuse and social disorganization.

This book will be of interest to students, researchers and academics in the fields of criminology, political science, environmental sociology, and natural resources.

Paul B. Stretesky is Professor at the School of Public Affairs at University of Colorado, Denver.

Michael A. Long is Assistant Professor at the Department of Sociology at Oklahoma State University.

Michael J. Lynch is Professor at the Department of Criminology at University of South Florida.

New Directions in Critical Criminology
Edited by Walter S. DeKeseredy, University of Ontario Institute
of Technology

This series presents new cutting-edge critical criminological empirical, theoretical, and policy work on a broad range of social problems,
including drug policy, rural crime and social control, policing and the
media, ecoside, intersectionality, and the gendered nature of crime. It
aims to highlight the most up-to-date authoritative essays written by
new and established scholars in the field. Rather than offering a
survey of the literature, each book takes a strong position on topics of
major concern to those interested in seeking new ways of thinking
critically about crime.

THE TREADMILL OF CRIME

Political economy and green criminology

*Paul B. Stretesky, Michael A. Long
and Michael J. Lynch*

Routledge
Taylor & Francis Group

LONDON AND NEW YORK

First published 2014
by Routledge
2 Park Square, Milton Park, Abingdon, Oxon, OX14 4RN

Simultaneously published in the USA and Canada
by Routledge
711 Third Avenue, New York, NY 10017

Routledge is an imprint of the Taylor & Francis Group, an informa business.

British Library Cataloguing in Publication Data
A catalogue record for this book is available from the British Library.

Library of Congress Cataloging-in-Publication Data
Stretesky, Paul.
The treadmill of crime : political economy and green criminology /
Paul B. Stretesky, Michael A. Long and Michael J. Lynch.
  pages cm. – (New directions in critical criminology)
1. Offenses against the environment. 2. Criminology--Economic aspects.
I. Long, Michael A. II. Lynch, Michael J. III. Title.
HV6401.S77 2013
364.1'45–dc23   2013002740

ISBN 978-0-415-65735-8 (hbk)
ISBN 978-0-415-65736-5 (pbk)
ISBN 978-0-203-07709-2 (ebk)

Typeset in Bembo
by Cenveo Publisher Services

CONTENTS

ILLUSTRATIONS

Figures

Table

ACKNOWLEDGEMENTS

The authors would like to thank Christine, Denver, Kelsey, Liz, Mason, and Vincent. Yes, we know we work too much and that an acknowledgement of thanks doesn't make up for lost time. We would also like to thank the International Green Criminology and Ecological Justice Working Group for providing us with meaningful professional interactions. When we say "green criminology," you don't laugh.

PBS, MAL, MJL

1

INTRODUCTION

Historically, criminologists have viewed the study of environmental harm as beyond the purview of the discipline. Today, however, studies of environmental harm are more frequent (Agnew 2011; Brisman 2008; Ellefsen *et al.* 2012; Eman *et al.* 2009; Gibbs *et al.* 2010; Lynch *et al.* 1989; Nurse 2013; Situ 1997; South and Brisman 2012; Stretesky 2006, 2008; Szasz 1986; Westerhuis *et al.* 2013). Nevertheless, studies within criminology that focus on zenvironmental harm are still rare.

A concerted effort to draw criminological attention to environmental harm emerged within criminology in 1990 when Lynch issued a call for "green criminology". According to Lynch, the study of crime failed to account for the tremendous amount of environmental harm that was occurring. Specifically, Lynch observed that criminologists failed to explain ecological destruction because they omitted social economic factors that shaped laws and power relations, and instead relied on the narrow definition of crime contained within the criminal law. In order to change this condition and explore the structural forces that lead to environmental harm Lynch (1990) argued that criminology needed a "green" emphasis. Building on that proposal, Lynch and Stretesky (2011a: 2) noted that the purpose of green criminology is to

> provide a space within criminology to examine the nexus
> between environmental problems, the definition of harms

against nature as crimes, the need to reconsider criminal justice practice and policy in relationship to the environmental harms they produce, the variety of victims environmental offenses create (for human and non-human species, as well as ecological segments such as wetlands, forests, air, and land, etc.), and the effect of environmental toxins on ecological systems and species' health and behavior.

Importantly, Lynch (1990) pointed out that a green criminological perspective should be radical and built on theories of political economy. It is this perspective on green criminology that shapes the focus of this book on exploring the political economy of green crimes.

Over the past 20 years, the study of green criminology has broadened significantly. Here, we focus on one dimension of green criminology, the production of ecological harms. As a result, for the purpose of this work we define green crimes as *acts that cause or have the potential to cause significant harm to ecological systems for the purposes of increasing or supporting production.* This definition encompasses behaviors that (1) produce harm that are already defined as crime by the state in the form of administrative and regulatory law *and* (2) those behaviors that are not criminalized, but which scientific evidence suggests may cause significant ecological destruction. This definition also includes harm to humans and animals produced by ecological additions, withdrawals and other forms of exploitative production practices. Omitted from our specific definition of green crime are the forms of street, white-collar, corporate, state crime, and corporate-state crimes that do not directly cause ecological destruction.

As noted, studies of environmental harm are becoming more frequent, while at the same time the examination of a green political economy of crime has largely been ignored. Much green criminology employs more traditional explanations and examinations of environmentally related crime. While the focus on environmental crime and harm by criminologists is welcome, the neglect of green political economic explanations is problematic for two reasons that mirror popular views about environmental issues. First is the false assumption that green crime can be reduced with better technology and/or alternative forms of governance that allows "markets" to remedy environmental problems. This approach is preferred in the business world, and includes an argument that the free market can adequately address environmental problems (for a critique see Burns *et al.* 2008). Some (e.g., Savitz 2006) argue that corporations have developed new environmental and sustainability ethics based on "triple bottom line" analysis – the idea that corporate rewards are not simply *financial*, but also *social* and *ecological*. This produces the optimistic idea – one that is not supported by the historical impacts corporations have had socially or environmentally – that "green" or "sustainable" production can reduce ecological destruction (Mol 1995; Mol and Spaargaren 2000). In our view, this optimism is misguided if the economic system does not change. As an example, consider the effort to address climate change, which has been stalled by powerful corporate and political actors, especially in the US (Lynch *et al.* 2010). Moreover, this type of thinking directs attention away from exploring the political economic drivers of ecological destruction, and the observation that capitalism and ecological preservation must oppose one another in order for economic expansion to continue (Burkett 2007). As noted in the chapters that follow, the nature of capitalism does not allow technology to solve the problem of green crimes related to ecological destruction and disorganization.

Second, there is the false assumption that if environmental damage is not defined as criminal, no serious harm is occurring. This idea is reinforced within criminology by the orthodox definition of crime as a violation of the criminal law, which excludes environmental crimes since these acts are often defined as violations of other, non-criminal forms of law. In response, some criminologists have offered alternative definitions of crime, suggesting that an environmental crime is "an act in violation of an environmental protection statute that applies to the area (jurisdiction) in which the act occurred and that has clearly identified criminal sanctions for purposes of police enforcement" (Clifford and Edwards 2012: 114). While this definition of harm is appealing because it expands the definition of crime, it ignores forms of ecological damage that have yet to be recognized by environmental regulations as harms. In our view, green crimes are acts that produce ecological damage whether or not they are recognized in the law.

Scientific research in various fields (ecology, biology, medicine, epidemiology, zoology, and toxicology) plays an import role in objectively identifying dangerous ecological harms that the law fails to recognize (Lynch and Stretesky 2001, 2011b). The orthodox definition of crime, in contrast, is a social construction based on power relations influenced by politics. Thus, when criminologists use the criminal law definition of crime, they are accepting the subjective nature of the criminal law's construction of crime, its reflection of economic and political interests, and limiting the study of crime to street crimes. In contrast, we prefer an objective measure of ecological harm defined by scientific research. To be sure, scientific results are sometimes biased by economic interests (Egilman and Bohme 2005), and it is important to understand that fact when interpreting scientific research produced, for example, by corporations with an interest in denying that their products or behaviors produce ecological damage.

When studying environmental crimes, criminologists should also address why some of those harms are recognized legally as crimes while others are not. Such an analysis, we believe, necessitates the examination of political economy and how political economic relations shape the law. In this view, we believe that the use of the orthodox criminological definition of crime within green criminology legitimates the state's definition of environmental crime over the findings produced by scientific research on environmental harms and, as a result, we prefer a definition of green crime that focuses on *ecological disorganization*.

The purpose of this book is to explore the political economy of green crime using treadmill of production theory (ToP) as developed by Schnaiberg (1980; Gould *et al.* 2008). Schnaiberg's theory not only provides a comprehensive, radical framework that can aid in developing political economic explanations of green crime, it specifically focuses attention on the forms of ecological disorganization capitalism produces. In doing so, ToP theory illustrates how political economic forces that drive the ToP extract and convert nature's use values, and destroy the integrity of nature and its reproductive network (i.e., its ability to produce the conditions for life) in the process (Burkett 2007; Foster 2002; see Chapter 2). Prior to describing treadmill theory, however, we briefly examine major theoretical frameworks within environmental crime. Next we briefly draw upon ideas in ecology to help readers understand what we propose, and demonstrate why our position is unique.

Green criminology as orthodox criminology

Orthodox criminology contains several theories that focus on the etiology of crime and deviance. These theories rely on underlying assumptions about human nature and social life that cannot be scientifically tested. Despite this fact, criminologists typically regard these theories as "laws" that guide the discipline and adhere to these explanations of crime religiously despite evidence to the contrary (for an overview see Clifford and Edwards 2012; Edwards *et al.* 1996). Nevertheless, there is some reason to suspect that some orthodox explanations of crime are relevant to green criminology. While we favor a political economic approach, we suggest that existing orthodox explanations may contribute to green criminology and be encompassed within a political economic perspective that focuses on ecological disorganization. As we will demonstrate, recent work by Agnew (2011) helps explain our position with respect to orthodox theories of crime. In general, there are five major criminological theories that have been applied to environmental harm and crime that may be of potential use to exploring green crime.

Perhaps the most obvious orthodox explanation of crime that may have some utility is *deterrence theory* (Becker 1968; Zimring and Hawkins 1973: Kennedy 2012). The concept of deterrence is found in the economics literature and has been largely copied by criminologists (see Gunningham *et al.* 2005). Deterrence is often regarded as a general theory of crime that can be applied to any type of criminal behavior (Cornish and Clarke 1987). The idea is that people acting individually and together in organizations (such as corporations) act rationally, and in so doing, respond to pleasure and pain, which can be employed to guide behavior by maximizing pleasure and minimizing pain (Becker 1968). Deterrence theory suggests that punishment for violations of environmental law will decrease criminal behavior because actors will not want to be punished again (specific deterrence), and because their punishment sends a strong message to other actors that they too will be punished if they violate the law (general deterrence). Thus, the notion that environmental crime can be deterred is based on the characteristics of punishment. Specifically, if punishment is swift enough and the offender can link it to the crime, and the punishment is certain and of the appropriate severity, it can be employed to deter any form of law violation (Bailey *et al.* 1974). Because deterrence theory assumes that offenders are similar, the focus of deterrence theory is on the crime, laws, and enforcement. Thus, the assumption is that environmental laws need to be modified to prevent environmental crime.

Unfortunately, there are empirical problems with the argument that deterrence reduces crime. First, while some environmental crimes may be punished and deterred, power interests ensure that not all forms of environmental harm are considered for punishment under the law. Thus, the most serious damage may be left unaddressed by the state. In fact, a vast majority of ecological damage is allowed under the law and in some instances encouraged through corporate profits and returns on investments (through tax dividends, for instance). In such situations there may be more of an incentive to increase natural resource consumption and toxic releases. It is for precisely this reason that deterrence does not do a very good job of reducing ecological harm.

Second, deterrence messages are also not likely to be certain or swift. Legal battles over large-scale pollution are sometimes held up indefinitely, while the lack of environmental crime investigators reduces the probability of detection. Some companies create plans to limit their liability, which decreases the certainty of punishment. In short, there is likely to be little reason to expect that environmental deterrence can completely eliminate crime, and even less reason to suspect that it will have much impact, if any, on ecological destruction.

Finally, there are other considerations that prevent deterrence from being successful. Many individuals and organizations are not rational and it may be the case that the normative culture within an organization filters deterrent messages and is more important than deterrence itself (Gunningham *et al.* 2005; Thornton *et al.* 2005). Thus, while few criminologists have applied deterrence theory to environmental crime (Stretesky 2006), the extent to which punishment may prevent that environmental crime or harm has been confirmed by economists (e.g., Gray and Shimshack 2011). Nevertheless, as we have previously noted, the role of deterrence in preventing ecological disorganization is highly questionable.

Related theories that also draw upon the rational choice perspective include *situational crime prevention and routine activities theory*. Both assume that offenders are not only rational actors, but motivated to commit crime. Routine activities theory (Cohen and Felson 1979) suggests that crime can be predicted by examining how three elements converge in space and time: motivated offenders, suitable targets, and the absence of capable guardians. Situational crime prevention involves crime reduction "measures directed at highly specific forms of crime that involve the management, design, or manipulation of the immediate environment in as systematic and permanent way as possible" to prevent crime (Clarke 1983: 225).

Routine activities and situational crime prevention explanations have some potential implications for green criminology, but focus largely on individuals and individual profit-making. For instance, Pires and Clarke (2012) examined how situational crime prevention and routine activities explain parrot poaching in Mexico. Other studies of poaching and natural resource crimes have also drawn heavily on situational crime prevention theories (Lemieux and Clarke 2009; Pires and Clarke 2011). Because many people see the lack of capable guardians as a significant issue in ecosystem destruction, non-profit organizations have emerged to monitor fragile ecosystems and offending corporations and, thus, act as capable guardians that may prevent environmental harm and crime (Knight and Stretesky 2011). Situational crime prevention shows promise for combating ecological disorganization and environmental crime precisely because many non-profit organizations do not accept the state's definition of crime and instead define crime as harmful actions to ecosystems. In many instances, however, the behavior of the guardians is defined by the state and society as criminal, especially when activist organizations interfere with production (Gottschalk 1999; Ellefsen 2012). As we will demonstrate, many organizations work to provide monitoring efforts to supplement state resources and shame organizations into environmental compliance by threatening corporate profits through halting production.

A third orthodox criminology explanation that has been used to examine environmental crime is *self-control theory* (Gottfredson and Hirschi 1990). This theory has dominated criminological discourse since the 1990s and suggests that individuals who are not properly socialized by their parents have low self-control and therefore are more likely to participate in crime and deviance. Individuals with low self-control engage in crimes that involve considerable risk and are both impulsive and physical. Gottfredson and Hirschi (1990) note that the theory should also apply to corporate offending, including environmental crime. Following that assumption, Ray and Jones (2011) note that characteristics associated with low self-control such as some psychopathic traits are associated with the intention to dump toxic waste.

In our view, the low self-control explanation has several limitations. For instance, the ability of the theory to explain corporate damage to the ecosystem is wanting because organizational context and socialization must be considered. In short, individuals are socialized within organizations to behave in ways that may damage the environment in order to achieve organizational goals and increase production (Pearce and Tombs 1998). In addition, many corporate officials have high levels of discipline and are committed to their organizations. This discipline and commitment often promote environmental offenses within the organization. Thus, corporate discipline and commitment, not low self-control, places individuals in a position where they can do significant damage to the ecology. As Reed and Yeager (1996: 357) observed, "we as often find committed employees breaking laws on behalf of purposes to which the work group is loyal and upon which they are dependent, and which have been rendered as morally superior to those inscribed in law". We also suggest that self-control theory is unable to explain trends in environmental harm because the focus is on individuals and not the economic structure. If individual self-control were the main cause of ecological disorganization, it becomes difficult to explain the tendency for environmental crime related to ecological disorganization to increase over time, as it is unlikely that there is a global explosion of individuals with low self-control. In short, we argue that the question is not "What causes an individual (or set of individuals) to engage in acts that harm the environment?" Instead, the more important question is: "How does the organization of society promote an increasing level of environmental harm?"

A fourth popular criminological theory that has been applied to environmental crime is *social learning theory*. As initially developed by Sutherland (1949), social learning theory has been used to examine environmental harm and crime (see also Akers 2009; Bandura 1986). Social learning suggests that individuals learn to become criminal through their interactions with significant others (e.g., parents, siblings, teachers, and peers). Thus, offenders learn the rationalizations and motives for becoming criminal as well as the techniques for carrying out their crimes. Research on conservation-related crimes and animal cruelty suggests this might be the case (Sollund 2011). In addition, it is likely that children learn various forms of destructive environmental behavior and rationalizations for that behavior from their parents (Barraza and Walford 2002). Nevertheless, the idea that the majority of environmental crime is learned through primary interactions with others is not likely, and disregards opposing effects such as the expansion of environmental education curriculum or the influence of the media (Leeming *et al.* 1995). Since environmental harm is largely a result of production, not consumption, those individual education programs designed to make people more aware of their impact on the environment are unlikely to change production practices that drive the current ecological crisis. This is because schools and other social institutions often socialize students in orthodox economics – the very type of economics that emphasizes increasing levels of production that harm ecosystems and the biosphere. And, while consumptive behavior does have environmental impacts and is likely to be learned, production, not consumption, is the locus of environmental harm. Thus, social learning theory may be useful for explaining modest amounts of environmental harm within the current social structure, but environmental education alone is not going to prevent the increasing levels of ecological disorganization observed today.

Finally, *strain theory* is another orthodox criminological explanation that has been applied to environmental harm and crime by Robert Agnew. Agnew's version of strain theory focuses on individual rather than social structural strain, and he has recently applied that idea to explore the relationship between climate change and crime (Agnew 2012). Agnew (2011) hypothesizes that strain, reductions in social controls, beliefs favorable to crime, and criminal traits are all *outcomes* of climate change. He specifically proposes that "there is good reason to believe that climate change will become one of the major forces driving [street, state, and corporate] crime as the century progresses" (Agnew 2012: 21). It is climate change that will create individual sources of strains such as food and freshwater shortages, as well as natural disasters and other extreme weather events that lead to malnutrition, disease, unemployment, and migration, that in turn lead to street crime. Moreover, typical street crime will increase because families will be disrupted through higher levels of disease and illness as well as migration and job loss, and therefore not be able to exercise adequate levels of social control over youth (Agnew 2012: 32). Furthermore, Agnew (2012: 33) notes that as the state is increasingly unable to meet the needs of people, it will create an environment where there are more beliefs favorable to crime, and mental disorders may increase as a result of "poor parental bonding and supervision, low levels of stimulation, stressful experiences, and/ or poverty." The idea that changing ecological conditions produce strains that may generate individual-level deviant and criminal behavior is interesting, but it is irrelevant as an explanation of ecological disorganization. Moreover, individual-level strain theory fails to explain why those social groups that experience the most strain are likely to view environmental crime as more serious than street crimes (Shelley *et al.* 2011), and are less likely to engage in acts that cause the most ecological destruction (Simon 2000).

Two important observations can be made with regard to how current orthodox explanations of crime apply to green crimes. First, most orthodox explanations of crime fail to adequately explain green crime. This is true because most explanations of crime were created and applied to individuals who commit street crimes, who are poor, undereducated, and live in disorganized neighborhoods with deficient social capital and social support. These explanations also omit an important issue – the effect of law-making on traditional measures of crime. That is, because criminologists define crime as a violation of law, and interest groups affect the construction of environmental law, environmental laws are not a good means of identifying the scope and extent of environmental harms that occur in society, such as ecological disorganization. Worldwide, ecological disorganization is increasing. Yet, the law often ignores the harms corporations do to the environment and the identification of those harms in the scientific literature. Thus, to explain and understand green crime, it is necessary to look beyond the discipline of criminology.

Second, while orthodox criminological explanations may have a role to play in explaining green criminology, those kinds of explanations are of secondary importance to structural explanations capable of conceptualizing and describing the widespread nature of green crimes, such as political economic theory. Thus, there is sufficient reason to move beyond orthodox explanations of crime to explain green crimes.

Importance of ecology

The underdevelopment of political economic explanations of green crime, combined with the weaknesses of orthodox explanations of environmental harm, lead to our examination of ToP theory as an alternative explanation for green crimes. In our view, ToP provides a useful political economic explanation for green crimes, and a theoretical framework for green criminology. In order to examine this framework in greater detail, we turn our attention to explaining some important concepts used throughout our work.

Most important is our use of the terms "ecology" and "ecosystem." Ecology, as noted in Chapter 2, is the study of organisms and their relationships within the environment (Walker 2012). As Walker notes, ecologists draw attention to these relations at different levels of analysis, including individual organisms, entire ecosystems (composed of a variety of organisms and non-living components), and groups of ecosystems and transitional zones between ecosystems (e.g., our biosphere). Because natural resource extraction and pollution can impact ecosystems on various levels, ecologists may examine the relationship that pollution has on individual organisms, groups of organisms, ecosystems, or the biosphere.

An important concept in ecology is the transfer of energy through the ecosystem. Walker (2012: 84) notes that the flow of energy through the ecosystem is generally linear and originates in the sun. As noted in Chapter 2, the sun's energy is converted to carbon-based energy by plants. This energy takes carbon-based forms and is consumed by animals that die and decompose and then provide the necessary nutrients for plants to thrive in the ecosystem. Energy is important because it is constantly converted by nature and because it helps explain the carbon cycle. In the carbon cycle, primary producers convert sunlight into energy and simultaneously remove carbon dioxide from the atmosphere and convert it into carbon. Disrupting this carbon cycle may cause significant change in, or destroy, an ecosystem, a phenomenon currently unfolding in the form of climate change (Walker 2012). Several other cycles exist and help maintain ecosystems, including the nitrogen cycle, the phosphorus cycle, and the sulfur cycle. All of these are threatened when pollution is released into the environment (Foster *et al.* 2010). The relationship between energy, primary producers, and natural resource withdrawals and additions is examined in detail in Chapters 2 to 4.

Organization of book

We have organized our work on green crime around ToP theory. Thus, the book explores major concepts in ToP, in addition to an application of ToP to examine various green crimes.

Treadmill of production

Chapter 2 examines ToP theory and its relevance to green criminology. We note that both green criminology and ToP theory can benefit from additional focus on the law. Specifically, we examine the major assumptions and scope of the theory. Our focus is largely on trends in production that provide support for that theoretical perspective. We define the concept of ecological disorganization, as that is central to the notion of green crime. Moreover, we present some evidence that suggests that production is increasing.

Crimes of withdrawals and additions

It is important for green criminologists to identify the harm associated with ecological disorganization (Lynch and Stretesky 2001). Chapters 3 and 4 organize this analysis by dividing crimes associated with ecological disorganization into (1) ecological withdrawals and (2) ecological additions. Doing so also draws attention to green victims and victimization produced by ecological withdrawal and addition processes. The British Petroleum (BP) oil spill in the Gulf of Mexico is an example of a well-publicized catastrophe that caused significant ecological disorganization and resulted in BP pleading guilty to 14 criminal counts. Viewing BP as a "bad apple" corporation ignores the larger social and economic forces that lead to such incidents. In a treadmill perspective, BP and other energy-producing firms can be interpreted as connected and embedded in the treadmill and are hence influenced by treadmill factors such as the drive to expand profits and production. Viewed in this way, BP's location in the ToP allows us to see these crimes as *social problems* as opposed to *personal troubles* or isolated events (Mills 1959). In doing so, the ToP framework allows us to uncover patterns of crime and deviance linked to the treadmill, and to focus responses to crimes of ecological disorganization on policy solutions that generate structural changes in the treadmill, as opposed to isolated solutions aimed at individual offenses committed by a given corporation. For example, simply placing restrictions on oil drilling in the Gulf will not remove the pressure to expand energy extraction or lessen the forms of ecological disorganization associated with energy extraction. In recent years, for example, a number of oil spills have occurred in the US, indicating that this problem is much more widespread than the oil spill in the Gulf (Burgherr 2007). As one specific example, consider that the oil spill occurring at Taylor Energy Wells from Platform 23051 has been underway since September 16, 2004! More recently, the expansion of hydro-fracturing technology to recover natural gas in the Midwest, Mid-Atlantic, and Northeastern US states poses significant environmental consequences (Linley 2012). The consequences of these ecologically destructive extraction and production technologies are a social problem that is not addressed simply by focusing attention on responding to these adverse outcomes after they occur.

Studying ecological crimes of addition and withdrawal also allows examination of the ways in which the legal system perpetuates and shapes green crime and the definition of environmental crime, by referencing concepts such as the social construction of crime as it relates to the treadmill and the interests of treadmill actors (Quinney (2008 [1970]). While orthodox criminology continues to focus attention on the crimes of the poor and powerless and controlling those behaviors (Reiman 2007), it ignores the much more significant crime and justice issues related to ecological disorganization that are of concern in green criminology.

To be sure, in some instances ecological harms related to withdrawals or additions are defined as criminal to legitimize law (Lynch and Stretesky 2003: 219). The social construction of crime perspective helps explain why some environmental laws place constraints on powerful actors. In discussing this issue, Gould *et al.* (2008) note that state regulations tend to favor treadmill institutions over citizen organizations. Thus, green criminologists should examine not only organizations that violate laws, but also the construction of environmental laws that define harm as crime, as well as actions that cause significant environmental harm but are not defined as crime (see Agnew 2011). As noted, we adopt this approach when we examine crimes associated with ecological withdrawals in Chapter 3 and crimes of ecological additions in Chapter 4. Within those chapters we attempt to identify the circumstances under which these harmful behaviors are allowed to persist without being defined or treated as criminal. In short, we ask how systems of production shape systems of justice, by focusing specifically on environment (White 2008).

Social disorganization and ecological disorganization

While ToP theory has not addressed the issue of street crime, the theory lends itself readily to a structural explanation of the etiology of ecological crime. This issue is explored in Chapter 5. For example, as chemical technology increases and displaces workers from production, expanding the rate of surplus value and unemployment (Lynch and Michalowski 2006), the treadmill produces forms of social injustice that can be examined as crimes against the environment (in the form of ecological disorganization) and as crimes against the working class. This kind of production-related social disorganization has been described by Rifkin (1995: 30) in relation to agricultural production:

> The rapid elimination of work opportunities resulting from technical innovation and corporate globalisation is causing men and women everywhere to be worried about their future. The young are beginning to vent their frustration and rage in increasingly antisocial behaviour. Older workers, caught between a prosperous past and a bleak future, seem resigned, feeling increasingly trapped by social forces over which they have little or no control. In Europe, fear over rising unemployment is leading to widespread social unrest and the emergence of neofascist political movements. In Japan, rising concern over unemployment is forcing the major political parties to address the jobs issue for the first time in decades. Throughout the world there is a sense of momentous change taking place – change so vast in scale that we are barely able to fathom its ultimate impact.

To be sure, workers have faced oppressive conditions throughout history. The ToP has sped up that process, and more workers have found themselves unemployed and eventually enmeshed in the criminal justice system (Reiman 2007). As ecological disorganization intensifies social disorganization where treadmill processes are occurring, labor is being increasingly marginalized, perhaps expanding the likelihood that communities suffering from concentrated poverty experience crime, violence, and deviance.

Non-human crime and violence

ToP theory has implications for exploring non-human exploitation and violence. Within green criminology, animal abuse has attracted significant attention (Beirne 1999; Ellefsen *et al.* 2012; Nurse 2013), and green criminology has opened an academic space for criminologists to examine these issues. Much of that research has drawn inspiration from Beirne's (1999) non-speciesist argument that focuses attention on including non-human species as appropriate criminological subjects, and on moral and philosophical approaches such as the one proposed by Benton (1998). However, research has not examined the problem of animal abuse in the context of the ToP, nor has treadmill theory addressed these issues in any serious way. Wildlife, for example, suffers from animal abuse when a wetland is destroyed or a wooded area is deforested, or a mountaintop is removed for the purposes of mining. Animals are also abused on corporate farms. While the latter form of animal abuse does not involve the kinds of environmental destruction that characterize the other example, these issues are all related to the ToP, an issue examined in Chapter 6.

Environmental enforcement organizations

ToP theory also has implications for green criminology and the control of green crime through the study of environmental justice and those citizen groups and organizations that are emerging to shape the definition of crime and enhance enforcement (Stretesky *et al.* 2010). Environmental justice movements and organizations attempt to remake environmental law and social control, and can be described as environmental policing organizations (Lynch and Stretesky 2013).

Treadmill research has devoted significant attention to environmental justice organizations (Gould *et al.* 1996).

Enforcement organizations engaged in advocacy and operations work (Knight and Stretesky 2011) are often international non-profit organizations that act independently from the government, and advocate for the stronger enforcement of environmental laws to protect the environment. These groups operate at local, national, and international levels and may lobby, denounce, and even influence states to act on environmental issues. In addition to advocating for stronger environmental policy and practices, environmental policing non-governmental organizations may take on an operations function to enforce or prosecute environmental crime (Knight and Stretesky 2011). For example, as discussed in Chapter 6, the Sea Shepherd Conservation Society engages in "confrontational tactics due to its sophisticated use of international law, and by taking advantage of overlapping international legal regimes" in order to prevent wildlife violations (Bondaroff 2011).

Treadmill theory has significant implications for green criminology by drawing attention to environmental organizations and their activities. Moreover, since these organizations can shift the "balance of power between activists, state regulators, and private firms based on their ability to contest official accounts of environmental quality" (Overdevest and Mayer 2008: 1497), they actively shape environmental law.

Chapter 7 draws attention to community environmental policing and its activation of community members to address the monitoring of environmental violations (Lynch and Stretesky 2013). In this view, community members are seen as having a stake in monitoring local environmental problems, and environmental enforcement authorities have increasingly relied on community members for such tasks despite the known limitations of this approach (O'Rourke and Macey 2003). Despite these limitations, extant research suggests that collaborative partnerships between environmental enforcement agencies and citizen's groups may improve environmental quality and enforcement efficiency (Cable and Benson 1993). ToP theory and green criminology both draw upon concepts of environmental justice in the case of enforcement. Many of these studies examine the unequal distribution of enforcement and the consequences of this enforcement for marginalized communities. We briefly review that overlap in Chapter 7.

We conclude our work in Chapter 8 with some observations about green crime and the future of green criminology. We note that there is much work to be done, especially as related to the development of both ToP and green criminology. It is toward that end that we now turn.

2

TREADMILL OF PRODUCTION FOR GREEN CRIMINOLOGY

Treadmill of production (ToP) theory helps explain how economy and ecology are related to green criminology. This chapter describes the scope, assumptions, concepts, causal processes, hypotheses, and relevance of treadmill theory for green criminology.

Scope

ToP theory, developed by Allan Schnaiberg, is described in detail in his 1980 work, *The Environment: From Surplus to Scarcity*, to explain how and why humans contribute to environmental problems. Schnaiberg's explanation focuses attention on the political economy of production and its relationship to environment harms (Schnaiberg 1980: 18). Political economy is a structural theory that draws attention to class relationships and structures, and when connected to Schnaiberg's ToP argument, can be employed to explore how class relations and structures affect ecological disorganization and environmental harms. In the early years, ToP theory focused on the intersection of political economy and environmental problems within the United States, but has since been extended into a global political-economic approach (Vail 2007; White 2008; Gould *et al.* 2008).

Assumptions

ToP theory relies on several important assumptions. The first assumption is that nature engages in production. As Schnaiberg (1980: 13) observes, "an ecological system ... has a production function [that] consists of the creation of living matter – biomass – by the process of birth, growth, and decay." Natural production follows the rules of nature, such as the laws of thermodynamics (Schnaiberg 1980: 13). First, based on the conservation of energy principle, *energy cannot be created or destroyed, only transformed*. Second, the law of entropy states that *as energy is transformed in production, it takes on less organized forms*. For example, when a tree is burned, the energy stored in that tree is released into the environment and the surrounding space warms (Schroeder 2000). The energy in the tree is transformed into heat and ash and the energy stored in the tree has become reorganized, or disorganized, in space. The implications of this assumption are far-reaching and shape our view of green criminology. As we will demonstrate, many green crimes occur as humans interfere with the ecosystems to produce commodities, and in so doing produce ecological disorganization through economic production.

Following the laws of thermodynamics, entropy is non-reversible. Thus, as energy changes from one form to another it becomes more evenly spread out through the environment and moves toward a state of equilibrium (Schroeder 2000). While it is hard to comprehend, at some point all production must end because total energy equilibrium is reached and no more energy can be transformed from one form to another. For example, if our sun were to run out of solar energy, the natural production of living matter on earth would cease as the earth, sun, and space surrounding them would eventually reach equilibrium (i.e., the same temperature). Many have argued that entropy is accelerated by capitalism and its constant expansion of production and consumption of energy for the purpose of accumulating wealth (Burkett 2007). And this explains why it is important to consider a political economic explanation for ecological disorganization.

These three assumptions (production, conservation, and entropy) are extremely important in ToP theory because, as Schnaiberg argues, humans have created an economic system (capitalism) that is altering the ecological system by disrupting the speed of naturally occurring entropy processes. Thus, the final major assumption of Schnaiberg's work is that *human economic systems interfere with the organization of ecological systems*, and Schnaiberg focuses specifically on capitalism as a significant cause of environmental disorganization. In this, Schnaiberg argues that the very dynamics of capitalism and its continual drive to expand production produced ecological disorganization.

Capitalism is the world's most dominant economic system, and because of its dominance the world's economic system is generally referred to as global capitalism (Greider 1998). A driving force behind capitalism is constant expansion of production to expand the volume of profit. In a capitalist system, access to ownership, especially the tools or means of production, are unequally distributed. While capitalists own the means of production, they need workers to operate the means of production. Luckily for the capitalist, in order to survive, the non-owners or workers must sell their labor power to the capitalist. That labor power is employed by the capitalist to convert raw materials into commodities. In order to create a profit from this system, the capitalist must manipulate the production process in ways that intensify labor and make it more productive so that labor produces surplus value. In the long run of history, labor is intensified and surplus value is produced by increasing the use of machine and chemical technology to replace human labor. In the long run, this produces marginalization of the workforce, and leads to growing unemployment and underemployment. This is a very general description of how capitalism works, and further details are provided by Marx (1976 [1867]). We are not the first researchers in criminology or environmental studies to link capitalism and crime (e.g., Foster 2002; O'Connor 1998; Quinney 1980; Reiman 2007) using these ideas.

As Magdoff and Foster (2011: 43) note, the goal of capitalism is to end up with more money after production, and the process of accumulation is seen as endless: capitalism "recognizes no limits to its own self-expansion – there is no amount of profit, no amount of wealth, and no amount of consumption that is either enough or too much." This assumption about production under capitalism is critical to Schnaiberg's theory of environmental disorganization. Because capitalism is driven to constantly expand, it also constantly expands its extraction of raw materials. The problem, however, is that the natural world is finite, and the expansionary tendencies of capitalism are not ecologically sustainable. In short, because continuous expansion of capitalist production is not ecologically sustainable, the normal development of capitalism produces continuous ecological disorganization and damage. That damage comes from the continuous *withdrawal* of raw materials from nature and the pollution associated with both the withdrawal and production processes.

Important concepts and variables

Ecological disorganization

The term "ecosystem" is used to describe the set of relationships between organisms and their environment (Odum and Barrett 2004: 5). ToP theory suggests that capitalism interferes with ecosystems in a way that disorganizes the ecology, and changes the relationship between organisms and their environment, and the concept of *ecological disorganization* occupies an important place in ToP theory. In ToP theory, the primary cause of ecological disorganization in the modern world is capitalism. Ecological disorganization occurs because capitalist production negatively impacts the relationships between organisms and their environment and impacts the self-sufficiency of the earth's biological system (e.g., Lovelock and Margulis 1974; Lovelock 2007). We examine how these harms occur in more detail in Chapter 3.

In short, the greater the impacts of production on ecosystems, the greater the level of ecological disorganization. In Schnaiberg's view, capitalism's drive for continuous expansion must also accelerate ecological disorganization, and has a tendency to do so at ever greater rates. It is important to point out that even as capitalists talk about environmental sustainability and achieving environmental stability through green technology, production continues to increase, which drives ecological disorganization. As Gould *et al.* (2008: 80) point out:

> In theory, green technologies could reduce the rate of ecological disorganization. Such a radical redirection of technology is

not likely to occur, however. Structured incentives for the large private capital interests that fund, organize and direct technological innovation will remain unchanged. Return on investment, not long-term protection of ecosystems, dominates as the decision criterion.

As a result, ToP theory suggests that the expansion of green technology, because of its ties to capitalist economic expansion, is not a cure for ecological disorganization.

To illustrate this point we draw upon the United States automobile industry, which is sometimes described as moving toward ecologically friendly production (Mikler 2009). The production of fuel efficient vehicles bolsters these claims. According to Figure 2.1, trends in fuel efficiency technology have improved considerably between the years of 1975 and 2011 (see Burns and Lynch 2004 for extended discussion).

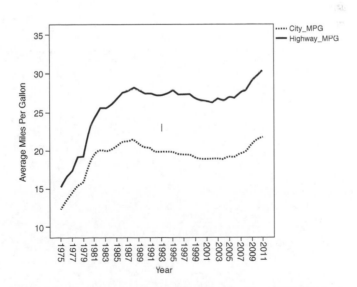

FIGURE 2.1 Fuel economy in miles per gallon for cars, 1975–2011
Source: US Environmental Protection Agency (2012)

Newer automobiles are much more efficient than they were 30 years ago. The average car built in 1975, for instance, obtained 12.3 mpg/city and 15.2 mpg/highway, compared to 21.7 mpg/city and 31.4 mpg/highway for 2011 vehicles (US Environmental Protection Agency 2012). The use of technology to improve efficiency is impressive, but unfortunately does little to decrease ecological disorganization. Why?

There are three reasons. First, as Figure 2.2 illustrates, there are now more vehicles on the road than there were in 1975, and more vehicle miles are driven. The United States Department of Transportation (2012) estimates that Americans drove *65.6 billion miles more* in 2011 compared to 1990. This represents a significant increase in gasoline consumption, even as green technology simultaneously decreased gasoline use in individual automobiles by increasing efficiency. As Figure 2.3 demonstrates, between 1975 and 2010 transportation-related oil consumption in the US increased by

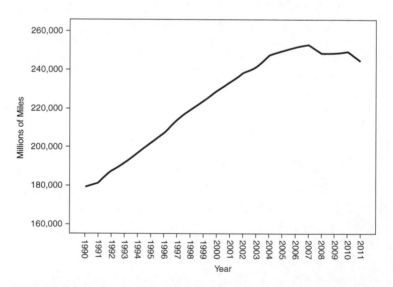

FIGURE 2.2 Average monthly vehicle miles driven in the US, 1990–2011
Source: US Department of Transportation (2012)

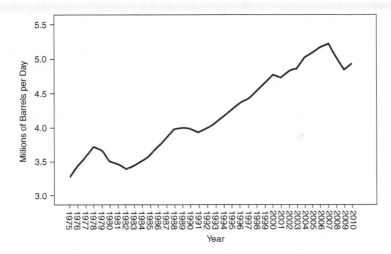

FIGURE 2.3 US petroleum consumption in the transportation sector, 1975–2010

Source: US Energy Information Administration (2011), Table 3.7c

53 per cent – from 3.2 to 4.9 million barrels/day (US Energy Information Administration 2012a). This consumption of oil for gasoline in the United States is closely tied to global production trends (Stretesky and Lynch 2009), forcing the United States to import much of its oil. Figure 2.4 shows that even while automobile technology has improved considerably, on a global scale, oil production increased rather than decreased. In 1975 the world produced around 55 million barrels per day, while in 2011 the figure was nearly 85 million barrels per day. In short, ecological disorganization associated with oil extraction and use is increasing, despite the implementation of green technology.

Second, some green technologies that are used to improve vehicle efficiency are extremely destructive to the environment. For example, special alloys are mined to create lightweight vehicles that use less gasoline (Cáceres 2007), creating ecological disorganization and shifting it to a different stage in the production process (Orsato *et al.* 2002). This makes other solutions to reducing oil consumption such as redesigning cities and transportation alternatives more feasible.

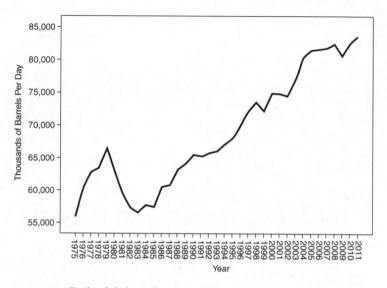

FIGURE 2.4 Daily global production of oil, 1975–2011
Source: British Petroleum (2011)

Third, people buy a greater number of cars today than in the past, generating increased ecological disorganization with respect to expanded raw materials extraction and energy use to produce those automobiles. For example, on average, about 16 million cars have been sold in the US annually since 1990. Consequently, while green technology improves fuel efficiency it does not necessarily decrease overall levels of environmental pollution, since the number of units produced remains the same over time (Gould *et al.* 2008). These examples illustrate how capitalism's drive to increase production and consumption can produce environmental disorganization even in the face of advances in green technology.

Additions and withdrawals

Schnaiberg's work challenged explanations that environmental problems were/are caused or cured by population levels, technology, and consumption. Instead the focus is on the environmental effects of expanded production under capitalism. While technology may slow ecological disorganization, it cannot prevent environmental destruction because capitalism requires ever-expanding production. Schnaiberg (1980: 23) develops two important concepts that explain how the transaction between the economy and ecology harm the environment: ecosystem withdrawals and ecosystem additions. Together, withdrawals and additions can be considered the source of ecological disorganization and are also central to organizing green criminology. Chapters 4 and 5 describe the implications of these ideas for examining environmental crime and deviance.

The withdrawals of natural resources from the ecosystem are necessary for production, and are transformed into products to be sold in the marketplace. As noted in Chapter 3, these withdrawals may give rise to a variety of crimes and deviance. While ToP theorists are careful to point out that natural resource extraction rates have generally decreased in the United States and other developed countries, they are offset by the expanded natural resource extraction in developing countries (e.g., oil and timber extraction) as capitalists seek the cheapest available natural resources. As Figure 2.4 illustrates, global oil production has increased while, as shown in Figure 2.5, US oil production has decreased considerably (US Energy Information Administration 2012a). In 1980, for example, the US produced about 8,597,000 barrels of crude oil, but only 5,672,560 barrels in 2011 – a 34 per cent reduction. That decline in US productivity is offset by worldwide increases in oil production and the negative environmental consequences that accompany increased worldwide oil production.

This same trend can be seen in the case of other natural resources, like timber production. As Figure 2.6 illustrates, timber production in the United States has decreased annually since the late 1980s, while timber imports and timber consumption increased during that time (Smith *et al*. 2009: 72). These increases have come at the expense of other sources of timber throughout the world. As is discussed in Chapter 3, a significant portion of timber extraction is illegal and creates considerable environmental harm and contributes to ecological

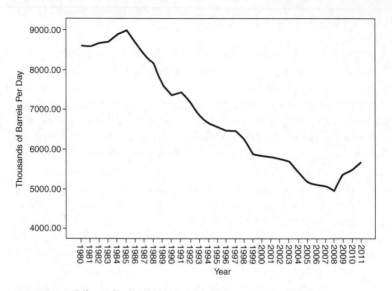

FIGURE 2.5 Oil production in the United States, 1980–2011
Source: British Petroleum (2011)

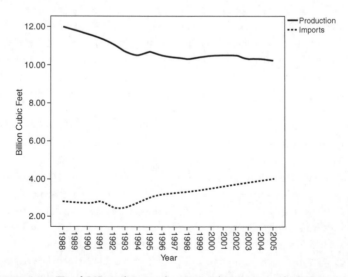

FIGURE 2.6 Total US timber production and imports in the US, 1988–2005
Source: Smith et al. (2009)

disorganization (Tacconi 2007a). The international criminal justice response to these crimes has been insufficient and non-state responses have emerged in the form of non-profit organizations (NGOs) that have begun to monitor these crimes while simultaneously calling for stricter environmental regulations (Global Witness 2007). The responses to the harms and crimes associated with ecological withdrawals are discussed in Chapter 6. The movement of ecological withdrawals, and thus, the changing patterns of environmental crime, to less developed countries is a consequence of the global economic relations or global political economy of capitalism. As Gould *et al.* (2008: 34) argue, "the globalizing of capital flowing from investors from industrial countries has been guided by cheap natural resources and weak environmental regulations." This situation promotes the growth of environmental crimes of withdrawal in less developed nations.

The addition of pollution to the ecosystem is also necessary for production under current production methods. These ecological additions come at various stages in the production process and, at the end of a life cycle, products are often discarded into the environment (Pellow 2000). ToP theorists suggest that ecological additions have become such a widespread form of corporate behavior that they seem ordinary and are often interpreted as the "price for progress" (Gould *et al.* 2008). These harms are ignored and not treated as crime until they cause an environmental catastrophe. However, their widespread scope is evident in the volume of environmental victimization. For example, more than 41 million Americans live within four miles of 1,134 Superfund waste sites – and millions more live near unlisted waste sites (Burns *et al.* 2008). Health hazards associated with exposure to chemicals found in these sites have been widely studied and demonstrate the human risks associated with these waste streams. A study of 593 sites in 339 US counties with hazardous waste groundwater contamination revealed increased levels of lung, stomach, intestinal, bladder, and rectum cancer (Griffin *et al.* 1989; Osborne *et al.* 1990).

On a global scale, in the mid-1990s the United Nations Environment Programme (UNEP) estimated that approximately 400 million metric tons of hazardous waste was generated annually worldwide, and this figure is likely much higher today (UNEP 2012). Illegal dumping and living close to Superfund sites are problems in the United States, but the outsourcing of production and the resultant transfer of toxic technologies and hazardous waste to the global south (South America, Africa and Asia), where environmental regulations are less strict, provide another avenue for the treadmill to continue to function unabated (Schutz *et al.* 2004). Moreover, as Gould *et al.* (2008: 43) note, the removal of large quantities of toxic waste from the global north to the south allows countries like the United States to trumpet improvements in domestic environmental indicators as if these were the result of cleaner and more environmentally friendly production processes, while much of the improvements are actually due to the relocation of production facilities to poor countries. Stretesky and Lynch (2009) examined this issue with regard to carbon emissions. They found that US imports were strongly associated with ecological additions (in the form of carbon) in the rest of the world. For example, consider the relationship between China's carbon emissions and their export of productions to the United States in Figure 2.7.

As data on carbon dioxide emissions in China indicates, a large volume of waste generated from the production process that is released into the environment appears to correspond with the export of products to the United States. As discussed in Chapter 4, the most economically and socially marginalized members of society are more likely to feel these ecological additions than wealthier citizens. Moreover, the enforcement of environmental laws related to additions may also be biased (Burns *et al.* 2008). Thus, as green criminology suggests, environmental crimes tend to target those victims that are the least powerful.

Another way to examine the concept of ecological withdrawals and additions is to tie them together through the use of ecological footprint measures (Wackernagel and Rees 1996). The ecological footprint is the calculation of the land and water area a human population uses to provide energy, food, and shelter, and includes measures of ecological withdrawals and additions (Wackernagel and Rees 1996). The footprint also adjusts for technology and population so

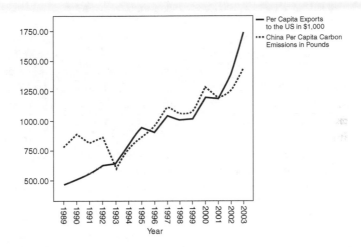

FIGURE 2.7 China's carbon emissions and exports to the US, 1989–2003
Source: Stretesky and Lynch (2009)

that it is only examining ecological disorganization. Data on the ecological footprint shows that over time, the footprint is increasing
faster than global population growth. For example, between 1961
and 2008 the global footprint increased from 2.4 hectares of land per
person to 2.7 hectares of land per person (Global Footprint Network
2012a). From 1961 to 2008, the world population increased by
118 per cent, while the per capita global footprint also increased, by
12.5 per cent. So, the population not only more than doubled, it
increased the resources withdrawn by 12.5 per cent. In 1961, the
world's 3.08 billion inhabitants had a global footprint of 7.4 billion
hectares, while in 2008, the world's population (6.7 billion) had
a total global footprint of 18.09 billion hectares, an increase of
145 per cent. This represents an enormous drain on the biosphere. In
fact, given the level of resources the world's population is using in
production, it is estimated that we need approximately 1.5 earths to
sustain current production practices. Thus, in financial terms we are
drawing down nature's capital. By the year 2050 it is estimated
that we will need nearly three earths to sustain production levels.

Because the level of natural resource production is declining as we increase production, the biosphere will not be able to sustain current production levels, even while technology innovations make production more sustainable (seen in the manifestation of global problems such as climate change). The idea that we are increasing the footprint is highly consistent with the treadmill analogy. That is, ecological disorganization is accelerating over time under capitalism.

It is important to point out that when examining the ecological footprint across countries, that footprint is not distributed equitably; it produces large-scale environmental injustices. For example, within the United States the average footprint is 7.2 hectares of land per person, while it is 4.8 hectares in the United Kingdom and France, 4.2 hectares in Japan, 3.3 hectares in Mexico, 2.2 hectares in China, 1 hectare in the Philippines, and 0.7 hectare in Rwanda (Global Footprint Network 2012b). The poverty and economic deprivation in Rwanda and other low-income countries demonstrate an inequality in production. As production increases, the material benefits of ecological disorganization go to high-income countries while those citizens living in low-income countries suffer from the economic and environmental consequences of that productive behavior (Schutz et al. 2004).

Labor, state, and corporate actors

ToP theory suggests that within the current economic system three groups of actors influence the relationship between the ecology and the economy and affect the extent of ecological disorganization over time. As Gould (1980) points out, each treadmill actor has an incentive to keep the treadmill running. The first set of treadmill actors are the producers or firms that engage in manufacturing by transforming extracted natural resources into products sold in the marketplace. As previously described, the current economic system constantly pushes these firms to increase production in order to survive. In short, for-profit firms are driven by the bottom line and promote production at the cost of environmental destruction (Gould et al. 2008). In many cases, international corporations locate production in countries with the lowest wages and weakest environmental laws in order to minimize the costs associated with the extraction of natural resources and production (Boyce 2002). In world system theory terms, these are the peripheral nations, and in the capitalist world economy those nations serve as valuable locations for cheap labor and raw materials employed by the core or advanced capitalist nations. Peripheral countries, which also tend to have small per capita ecological footprints, may be home to the most egregious types of environmental destruction that facilitate economic production and consumption patterns that benefit core nations. The products and raw materials created in these low-income countries, however, are exported to high-income countries for consumption. Because environmental regulations in low-income countries are non-existent, weak, or go unenforced, environmental crime, violence, and deviance are likely to emerge in the extraction of natural resources in those locations. These outcomes include those related to the health and safety of productive and extractive workers in peripheral nations. In many instances, the treatment of workers extracting natural resources in peripheral countries would be viewed as serious regulatory violations and crimes in the United States (Flynn 2005). Non-profit organizations that monitor workplace conditions in underdeveloped, peripheral nations have disclosed numerous instances of serious harm and death related to the production of commodities and the extraction of raw materials. These monitoring activities have also generated unexpected consequences and crimes. For instance, environmental activists that engage in monitoring efforts and other environmental struggles in peripheral nations have become the targets of violence and murder, sometimes at the hands of "company thugs" (Gerken 2012). In response, corporations have developed a variety of tactics to hide their behavior from the rest of the world, including hiring non-profit organizations to "green-wash" their destructive behaviors in order to divert attention away from their harmful practices (Greer and Bruno 1996).

Labor constitutes the second set of treadmill actors (Schnaiberg 1980). Like the corporations that employ them, labor is often motivated to support increases in production to promote job creation, wage increases and reduced unemployment. Capital, however, desires to increase production through the implementation of work-saving technology rather than expanded employment, yet promotes its expansion into undeveloped areas to enhance extraction and production by offering the promise of financial investment in areas that are economically depressed (Gould *et al.* 2008). Robert Bullard (1993) describes this situation as a form of economic blackmail because workers must accept environmental harm and lower wages, and some level of unemployment, in exchange for work.

Despite the negative consequences for the environment, labor unions may often support policies that increase production and accelerate ecological disorganization because those policies are beneficial to the short-term economic interests of workers. In reality, however, this benefit to workers is not realized over the long term, as technology generally displaces workers from production (Gould *et al.* 2008). For example, Stretesky and Lynch (2011) found that increases in coal production linked to mountaintop removal mining methods, as opposed to traditional forms of underground mining, are associated with a significant decrease in mining employment. This occurs because these techniques employ chemical and machine labor to replace miners.

The third major actor in ToP theory is the state. Like labor and corporations, the state often supports the expansion of production because it generates additional revenue in the form of taxes. Perhaps more important, however, is the influence of campaign contributions that state agents receive from corporations as an incentive to promote environmental regulations beneficial to corporations and the expansion of production (Schnaiberg *et al.* 2002). With respect to taxation, Woods (2006: 174) discovered that "political officials may be motivated to reduce regulatory stringency to gain a competitive advantage over their neighbors, thereby creating an aggregate movement toward the lowest common denominator." The state is also important in the study of criminology because it is the source of laws and allocates resources based on politics and finite resources (Walker 2006). As we note throughout the book, environmental laws, or the lack thereof, are connected to class and economic interests.

The state plays opposing roles in production. Bonds (2007), for example, suggests that when the treadmill is threatened by citizens and/or workers, the state may be forced to enhance environmental protection to maintain its legitimacy (Obach 2004; Wolfe 1977). In this sense, then, one of the key roles played by the state in the production process is its ability to influence the "speed" of the treadmill, which may occur when the state responds to citizen concerns over the pace of environmental destruction. Schnaiberg (1980: 249) suggests that "If the treadmill is to be slowed and reversed, the central social agency that will have to bring this about is the state, acting to re-channel production surplus in non-treadmill directions" (see also, Gould *et al.* 2008: 68). Thus, producer behaviors may be influenced by state regulation.

By drawing attention to these three sectors of actors, treadmill theory directs attention to social structure as a driving force behind ecological disorganization, and connecting social structure to the interests of participants in the production process. This allows ToP analysis to include agency-based explanations related to ecological disorganization, its shape and pace. An important set of actors, however, has been omitted from the discussion thus far: environmental organizations.

Environmental organizations

Environmental organizations, while not the primary focus of treadmill theory, constitute an additional set of actors that may pressure the state to create policies to reduce ecological disorganization. Thus, while corporations may pressure the state to promote environmental regulations that enhance economic production, environmental organizations can pressure the state to reduce ecological disorganization. The idea that environmental organizations can influence the state to change production practices is critical to notions of social change in ToP theory. Thus, environmental organizations remain one avenue for challenging ecological disorganization. Because some of these organizations struggle to shape definitions of environmental crime and aid in monitoring environmental crime and deviance, they are also relevant to green criminology (Knight and Stretesky 2011; Lynch and Stretesky 2013, 2010; Stretesky *et al.* 2010). There is some anecdotal evidence that citizen organizations have helped to reduce the negative externalities associated with production through their direct involvement in environmental problems and pressure on state actors. This has lead Gould *et al.* (2008) to argue that when workers and environmentalists join forces, they will be more effective in altering damaging ecological practices.

Causal processes and ecological disorganization

According to treadmill theorists, ecological disorganization intensified after World War II when production was sped up by significant increases in the volume of capital investment in new forms of chemical technology developed during the chemical revolution (Gould *et al.* 2008). These energy-intensive chemical technologies allowed workers to produce considerably more, leading to a decline in the price of commodities and an increased demand for commodities and the natural resources required to produce those products. These new chemically assisted production technologies also expanded the volume and the toxicity of waste being released into the environment (Gould *et al.* 2008), indicating that the new form of post-WWII capitalism was responsible for "expanding resource consumption and waste emissions" (York 2004: 355).

Consistent with the notion of continuous economic expansion, treadmill theory predicts that production must increase to pay off firm and stockholder investments in the development of chemical and energy-intensive technology that drives the post-WWII ToP (for criticisms, see Foster 2005). This produces a political economic system characterized by the continued expansion of "industrial production, economic development as well as increasing consumption" (Gould *et al.* 1996: 5). The theory is dynamic as it explains why ecological disorganization is increasing over time in relation to the treadmill's impact on the accumulation tendencies of capitalism, as well as the ideological belief that expanded production will advance public welfare.

The relevance of the treadmill to green criminology

ToP theory has had an important influence on environmental sociology (Buttel 2004), and has been incorporated into Marxist ecological explanations of environmental destruction (Foster 2005; Hooks and Smith 2005; Bunker 2005). Treadmill theory also has significant implications for green criminology, and several hypotheses and areas of work relevant to the study of green criminology can be developed by drawing upon treadmill theory.

Summary

ToP theory has made significant contributions to the study of ecological disorganization. The theory is based on a political economy of the relationship between economic production and ecological disorganization. The use of ToP theory is consistent with Lynch's (1990) call to develop a green criminology that draws on political economic theory. Integrating ToP theory and green criminology to explain the structural causes of environmental crime and to promote steady state environmental policies are critical if systems of justice are to adequately respond to environmental harm. Thus, the call for steady state environmental policies must focus on changing the economic base, as opposed to protecting one particular ecosystem or natural resource. Such policies also have implications for the criminological tradition rooted in social disorganization theory and the study of crime in general.

Schnaiberg (1980) argued that piecemeal environmental policies do little to alter the structure of production practices and have had insignificant long-term impacts on reducing ecological disorganization. Moreover, as we demonstrate throughout this work, these disjointed environmental enforcement activities do little to curb the problem of environmental crime and deviance. Since the economic system produces this disjointed criminal justice response to environmental harm, alternative solutions must be located. These alternatives include environmental justice movements and community environmental policing that can alter the balance of power and slow the ToP. Such pressure may be an important first step in promoting large-scale change. We take up these issues in the chapters that follow.

3

CRIMES OF ECOLOGICAL WITHDRAWALS

One of the driving forces behind capitalism is continuous expansion of the economy. The treadmill of production facilitates continuous economic expansion. However, in order to continuously expand production, the ToP must also expand its consumption of natural resources in the form of raw material and energy. In ToP, the raw materials and energy resources used in production extracted from the environment are referred to as ecological withdrawals. The extraction processes associated with these ecological withdrawals destroy the functioning of local ecosystems, and can contribute to the expansion of larger ecological problems, which together generate ecological disorganization. As the process of ecological withdrawal continues and expands, harms caused to local ecosystems accumulate and are magnified and contribute to global ecological disorganization.

The concept of ecological withdrawals has important implications for green criminology because it provides the context for explaining the consequences of ecological disorganization and the form and shape environmental laws acquire. Not all or even most of the ecological disorganization caused by ecological withdrawals are treated as crimes by environmental regulations. Green criminology draws attention to the question of why some withdrawals are defined as crimes while others are not, and how environmental law is constructed to reflect economic interests that maintain and promote natural resource withdrawals that facilitate the expansion of the ToP.

Orthodox criminology ignores these issues, and instead focuses its attention on street crimes and the construction of the criminal law. The construction of environmental laws related to controlling ecological withdrawals is much more complex than the construction of the criminal law. The issue of whether the environmental law recognizes green crimes related to ecological withdrawals involves a complex interaction between a variety of interests (economic, political, scientific, and social), each of which attempts to define the harms produced by ecological withdrawals. In this chapter, we employ two general examples to examine the construction of green crimes related to ecological withdrawals to illustrate these points: the extraction of timber/wood, and the extraction of fossil fuels. Before turning to those discussions, we review the concept of ecological withdrawal and the social construction of green or ecological crimes.

Ecological withdrawals

Ecological withdrawals represent one of the two major interactions between the ecology and the economy. Economic actors withdraw natural resources to create products that can be sold in the marketplace. These withdrawals take a variety of forms that can impact both "living and nonliving components of ecosystems" (Schnaiberg 1980: 24), and occur in ways that disorganize nature.

As an example, consider the withdrawal of energy from water. The energy stored in the movement of water from rivers to seas and oceans can be harnessed and converted to human use through large hydroelectric dams. As humans alter natural water patterns by building dams they may remove a primary energy source from the environment that carries the biogenic silica that reside in inland waterways, and thus adversely impact the marine phytoplankton that consume those silica for energy (Humborg et al. 2000). Phytoplankton are the ecological engine of the marine food system and supply the energy that powers ocean life. Phytoplankton help reduce carbon dioxide levels and combat global warming (Reynolds 2006). Large dams cause silica to precipitate from waterways, preventing them from reaching phytoplankton (Humborg et al. 2000). By disrupting the flow of water, dams disorganize the ecosystem and disturb the efficiency of the ocean's primary production unit. Simultaneously dams allow for the build-up of dead and decaying plant matter, and release carbon dioxide through both the production and consumption of electricity. International Rivers (2012) estimates that there are approximately 40,000 large dams in the world, several hundred of which are massive and stand over 150 meters (nearly 500 feet) tall. The legal system does not consider these kinds of ecological withdrawals problematic, and legal requirements such as environmental impact assessments are not required to take account of the harm dams cause to nature's economy and production. If this same kind of harm impacted economic production in a capitalist system, it would be reacted to harshly and defined as criminal (Spitzer 1975). In a green criminological perspective, with its emphasis on biological and ecological sciences, this damage to primary ecological units of production would be considered a crime against nature (Lynch and Stretesky 2011a; White 2008). In order to consider this issue in greater detail, we explore the social construction of crime. We then examine green crimes associated with the ecological withdrawal of timber/wood and fossil fuels, since these are a significant form of interaction between the economy and the ecosystem.

The social construction of green crime

The extraction of resources from the environment is an economic act that often produces significant environmental harm and disorganization. Society does not entirely ignore these harms, and has constructed rules to govern some forms of natural resource extraction. These rules typically favor capitalists' economic interests, tend to define extractive harms as acceptable so long as the extractors are not the poor (Marx 1842), and favor extraction over the preservation or conservation of resources (Foster 2011). These legal rules are not uniform and reflect historical and geographic variations in the distribution of the power of capital and the treadmill of production.

Criminologists recognize the existence of variation in the legal definition of crime by noting that crime is socially constructed

(Quinney 2008 [1970]). Radical criminology expanded on that concept by drawing on Marx's theory of capitalism to suggest that the social construction of crime in capitalist societies reflects capitalism's economic organization, and class power and conflict dynamics (Lynch and Michalowski 2006). Based on that view, we can suggest that environmental laws will be influenced by economic relations of production, and will consequently facilitate rather than place strict limits on environmental disorganization.

In orthodox criminology, the ecological disorganization that concern green criminologists is largely glossed over because orthodox criminology favors defining crime according to legal standards. For example, in the United States, the definition of crime found in most criminal justice textbooks is simple: "Crime is an intentional act in violation of the criminal law (statutory and case law), committed without defense or excuse, and penalized by the state as a felony or misdemeanor" (Tappan in Milovanović 2001: 78). Thus, omitted from the orthodox analysis of crime are significant harms caused by corporations that generate ecological disorganization. As radical criminologists point out, criminal law definitions are biased, tend to reflect class conflict, and promote a definition of crime focused on the behavior of the powerless (Lynch and Michalowski 2006). Following Quinney (2008 [1970]), it can be argued that the criminal law's social construction of crime is an act of economic and political power. As a result, the crimes identified in criminal law will tend to be those that disrupt the ideological frame of reference of capitalism, and consequently will tend to produce an image of crime as the work of the poor and powerless (Reiman 2007).

In contrast to the orthodox view, green criminology supports the contention that conflict and power are important to the definition of crime. As a result, green criminology reflects the observation that the social construction of ecological crime is shaped by the interests of powerful social actors and the structural dynamic of capitalism. This argument can be extended to the treadmill of production. In that interpretation, behaviors that harm the ecology that extend the economic goals of the ToP will tend to be unregulated or under-regulated. In this view, the presence or absence of environmental laws is an important *variable* in the treadmill of crime. If we extend Quinney's observations about social construction, for example, we can see that criminal law definitions will tend to exclude the harmful behaviors of economic elites. Extensive levels of ecological disorganization (withdrawals and additions) will not be defined as criminal even though those acts generate significant harm. To be sure, this is not always the case, as legitimation requires that the law appears fair and neutral, sometimes leading to the behaviors of the powerful being defined and treated criminally (Chambliss and Seidman 1982). This occurs rarely with respect to environmental crimes, which are often depicted as celebrated cases (Jarrell 2010). Environmental crimes will sometimes, however, be addressed by the state because citizen movements pressure the state to act (Jarrell and Ozymy 2010). Consequently, while the law primarily represents the interests of the powerful, it also contains mechanisms that allow it to retain legitimacy by appearing to control the behavior of the powerful.

This view of law and its relationship to power relations and the process of constructing crime helps explain how laws designed to control the behavior of the powerful, such as environmental laws, are possible. Because ecological withdrawals are central to production, they will often not be defined or treated as criminal even when they are extremely harmful. For example, new technologies of production such as hydro-fracking will tend to be tolerated even though they expand ecological disorganization. Sometimes, however, the reverse outcome occurs. For instance, as coal displaced timber as an important fuel source, the extraction of timber became more tightly regulated in some parts of the world. Thus, our central hypothesis in the case of ecological withdrawals is that ecological disorganization is prevented when environmental laws result in minimal disruption to economic expansion and profit-making.

This hypothesis calls for additional empirical work in this area, and for criminologists to pay greater attention to the relationship between environmental harm and the creation of laws that regulate or fail to regulate ecological disorganization. This chapter illustrates how the social construction of green crime will tend to reflect the importance of ecological withdrawals for production. Four examples of how this process emerges in natural resource extraction related to carbon-based energy are provided: timber/wood, coal, oil, and natural gas.

Timber/wood

At one time wood was a major fuel source in production, and was the primary fuel used in processes such as iron smelting in England (Ashton 1924; Hammersley 1973); it enabled the emergence of the industrial revolution. Wood was not only used for the construction of buildings, ships, and housing; it was also burned for cooking, heating, and as an industrial energy source. However, as wood became scarce in areas in proximity to industrial centers, this threatened the expansion of production. For instance, while iron ore was plentiful, there were not enough forests to transform iron ore into commodities. As a result of the limited availability of wood and its inefficiency in the production of iron, alternative methods of production were examined (Ashton 1924). Coal became the chief alternative not only for the production of iron, but as a fuel for steam engines. This technological advance in the extraction of heat from coal provided an alternative energy source that allowed production to continue to increase. The increased use of coal expanded coal extraction, which has ecological disorganizing effects, related to the destruction and pollution of nature, as well as long-term effects on climate change.

As forms of production changed, so did the social production of green crime. While there can be little doubt that timber management existed early in history, the impact of these laws is certainly debatable. For example, in Assyria in 700 BC the forests were preserved for the elite classes to hunt in leisure (Elliott 1996). There was forest management during medieval times in order to prolong production of timber (Elliott 1996). In short, historically laws that preserved timber as natural resources did exist, but were designed largely to ensure that production continued in a paradigm where people dominated nature (Elliott 1996). However, as many scholars note, these laws did not prevent the massive deforestation within industrial Europe that occurred as a result of such thinking (Elliott 1996).

Despite the continued use of forests for economic production, they have been increasingly recognized as an important natural resource needed to limit negative environmental outcomes such as climate change. As a result, efforts to protect forests from destruction have accelerated over time. At the same time, wood remains valuable to production as a raw material for products and sometimes as an energy source, and this means that timber laws will continue to be weakened by economic interests. While wood continues to play a significant role as a fuel source in the developing world, its availability in those regions has important implications for the survival of the poor (Naughton-Treves *et al.* 2007). In the modern context, international pressure to control deforestation as a response to climate change conflicts with capital's interests in the cheap supply of raw wood materials found in developing nations. In turn, capital's interest in those cheap raw wood materials can often impinge upon the ability of the poor to have adequate access to wood as a source of fuel. These competing interests in preserving and consuming wood shape laws related to, for example, logging across the nations of the world (Green *et al.* 2007).

Despite a recognition of the utility of protecting forests from destruction (since doing so reduces ecological disorganization and protects the ability of the ecosystem to reproduce itself and provide conditions that sustain life), the harvesting of timber continues to increase. As Kirilenko and Sedjo (2007) illustrate (see Table 3.1), timber production has increased in all areas of the world.

The importance of this table is that it shows that while timber production is continuously expanding, it has not expanded evenly across all countries that have timber stocks. Thus, poor and less developed countries are asked to forgo environmental laws that criminalize ecological disorganization so that the extraction of timber for the developed world can continue. This is the fundamental inequality or environmental injustice that emerges in the development of criminal laws as a result of treadmill of production policies. We examine the impact of this inequality and implications for ecological disorganization in detail below.

TABLE 3.1 Estimated trends in global timber production, 1965–2005 (billion m^3)

Year	Africa	Asia	Europe	North and Central America	South America
1965	310	810	300	480	150
1970	325	880	315	520	160
1975	350	925	310	525	180
1980	400	980	310	630	210
1985	440	1010	315	710	230
1990	490	1030	390	795	240
1995	550	1035	480	790	250
2000	590	1020	570	780	260
2005	620	1010	650	780	280

Source: Kirilenko and Sedjo (2007: 19700)

Every few years, the Food and Agricultural Organization of the United Nations (FAO) publishes a report, *The State of the World's Forests*. As the 2012 report indicates, deforestation is unequally spread across the nations of the world. The 2012 report estimates that from 1990 to 2010, about 3.3 percent of the world's forest has been lost, the wood being used for production, housing, fuel, and conversion into human development. While this seems like a small figure, the concern centers on the long-term impact of even these small changes on ecological disorganization. Forests, for example, take hundreds of years to sufficiently recover from ecological withdrawal (Bonnell *et al.* 2011; Liebsch *et al.* 2008). Logging activities may impact genetic diversity of tree species, meaning that forests may never completely recover from logging effects (Sebbenn *et al.* 2008). And, as science has firmly established, the loss of forest is associated with the ultimate form of ecological disorganization, global warming (Tacconi 2007b).

Efforts to regulate timber extraction and protect forests are complicated by the effects of international trade markets and how those influences affect indigenous peoples in developing nations. To restrain costs and enhance profit, capital shifts its resource extraction and production facilities across nations. Developing nations are often likely to have less restrictive environmental regulations to promote economic growth. When coupled with low wages, these less restrictive environmental laws reduce the costs of extracting raw materials in developing nations. The result is the export of significant quantities of raw materials to fuel the consumption patterns established in economically advanced nations, and a reduction in timber for the use of people in nations that are timber exporters. Wood and the charcoal made from wood, for example, are significant sources of domestic fuel in less developed nations, and thus when wood is exported from those nations, access to those sources of fuel for the poor around the world is restricted. Moreover, we must recognize that this form of economic resource extraction expands the scope of ecological disorganization across the face of the globe. The negative impacts of this process on rainforests that help regulate the earth's climate have expanded in recent decades, and are a factor that intensifies processes such as climate change.

The world system of production and consumption has important impacts on ecological disorganization and the distribution of the treadmill of production. In core nations such as the US, production has shifted from the use of wood as fuel to more abundant stores of coal. In core nations, the shift to these other energy sources allowed the law to provide stronger forms of protection for forests, and the number of forest protection laws in the US has expanded greatly as the importance of wood as a fuel source declined (Greene and Siegel 1994; Schnaiberg 1980). Many developing nations, however, tend to rely on wood as an energy source due to its availability, and are more likely to use wood-based charcoal as opposed to coal or oil in production. Lacking extensive laws that protect the environment, deforestation in these locations not only contributes to large forms of ecological disorganization such as climate change, but causes the price of wood to escalate and become unaffordable to the poor. The problem this presents is adequately addressing the ecologically destructive patterns of the extraction and use of fuel materials that promote ecological disorganization while simultaneously recognizing the rights of the poor to access fuel sources they need for survival.

This is no small matter, and efforts to address ecological disorganization must be sensitive to how those policies impact the poor.

Brazil provides an interesting example of this process. Large-scale metal manufacturing in Brazil remains wedded to the use of wood-based charcoal production. The production of charcoal in Brazil contributes not only to deforestation but also to poor air quality (Gomes *et al.* 2012). Generating the charcoal used in production, coupled with a focus on profit, has also lead to related crimes in Brazil such as the emergence of human trafficking to supply labor used to produce charcoal (Smith and Voreacos 2007). As one non profit representative reported, "slavery is endemic to the charcoal camps that supply the [steel] industry" (in Smith and Voreacos 2007: 1). In short, ecological withdrawals in the form of timber in Brazil have disorganized communities and created considerable human suffering. We address this issue more generally in Chapter 5. Moreover, given the importance of charcoal to commodity production, laws limiting the access of the population to wood and charcoal have emerged, and have become a particular hardship for the poor (Wyatt 2012). Economic profit and production pressures also impact the volume of illegal wood that is harvested to produce charcoal. Worldwide, Nature Conservancy (2011) estimates that approximately 32 million acres of natural forest are logged illegally. Recent estimates by Rhodes, Allen, and Callahan (2006) suggest that approximately 6 per cent of the global timber trade consists of illegal timber. This illegal timber is often imported into developing countries for production and to developed countries for consumption. Countries like Indonesia have large markets in illegal timber and some estimates suggest that as much as 70 per cent of Indonesia's timber exports are illegal (Nature Conservancy 2011). As the global economy continues to expand, we might witness a continued increase in timber production and expanded illegal timber in the marketplace to meet production demands.

Illegal timber extraction has been associated with state and corporate crime. For instance, illegal timber sometimes comes from countries with considerable levels of violence, conflict, and illegality, and because of those conditions is referred to as "conflict timber" (Rhodes *et al.* 2006). It has been suggested that these illegal sources of timber have been employed to finance terrorism and governments with extensive records of violating human rights (Salo 2004). In countries like Cameroon, Cambodia, Liberia, Burma, Zimbabwe, and the Democratic Republic of Congo, timber has been used to fund armed conflicts (Bannon and Collier 2003). In some instances, corporations take advantage of these situations and purchase cheap conflict timber from political leaders or rebels, facilitating their access to the financial resources required to maintain and expand violent conflicts. Logging companies operating in these countries may even engage in armed conflict in order to continue their ecological withdrawals. For example, Charles Taylor, the former President of Liberia, built his repressive political regime on natural resources, including timber reserves extracted from within his country. Global Witness (2002) reported:

> Taylor's increasing dependency on timber revenue has necessitated a desperate drive to maintain a firm grip on the industry. From 35 active concessions in 1999, the Forestry Development Authority granted only 25 companies the right to operate concessions in 2000. Of the 25 companies 10 are linked to arms trafficking and the formation of armed militias. These companies produced 583,231 cubic meters of logs in the first six months of 2000, more than 85% of the semi-annual production … it appears that Taylor [used revenue] to maintain his patronage system and to support notorious governmental and non-governmental paramilitary units guilty of various human rights abuses in the sub-region.

Enforcement agencies may sacrifice environmental enforcement to help preserve and conserve forests to maintain production where forests are central to production. For example, the palm oil industry is increasingly driving the Indonesian economy and represents as much as 5.6 per cent of that country's gross domestic product (Yusoff 2006). Palm oil is used in cooking and is produced in massive amounts. In order to produce palm oil, large portions of the forests in Indonesia and other major exporter countries are cleared and replaced by factory mono-crop farming (Koh and Wilcove 2008). As a result, biodiversity is decreasing (Koh and Wilcove 2008). Thus, where production is central to global economic interests, such as in the palm oil industry, the laws protecting forests take a back seat to economic interests, and ecological disorganization is intensified.

Forms of ecological disorganization associated with the withdrawal of timber are increasing globally. There are important connections between timber and crime that are relevant to the examination of ecological withdrawals within ToP theory. First, as production shifts from developed to developing countries, the number of laws that protect the forests in developed nations will expand. Despite this increased protection, global forest resources will continue to decline since the ToP shifts to developing nations, maintaining the ToP. Second, differential treadmill practices across nations promote timber crimes related to ecological disorganization such as illegal logging, links between conflict timber and state crime, the role of conflict timber in financing terrorism, and the use of illegal behaviors such as human trafficking to facilitate the withdrawal of timber from the environment. These crimes are being combated globally by non-profit monitoring organizations, as described in Chapter 7. Third, in developing nations, law will tend to follow production, outlawing the production of charcoal, for example, when it is not central to industrial production. However, as charcoal becomes less central to production, the behavior of the powerless will come to be defined as criminal, as they attempt to extract timber for use to produce charcoal as fuel merely to maintain their existence. Fourth, in developing nations where timber resources are more plentiful than in developed nations, environmental law will be less protective of timber extraction. This promotes the export of timber products from developing to developed nations, and the enhancement of ecological disorganization in developing nations.

Fossil fuels

Fossil fuels are important modern energy sources; when burned, they release large quantities of energy. Nevertheless, the withdrawal of fossil fuels causes significant ecological disorganization and ecological destruction. The next chapter examines the consequences of the release of carbon dioxide into the environment as an ecological addition. Here, we examine the harm and laws associated with the extraction of coal, oil, and natural gas – three major sources of energy in the global economy. We expand upon the ecological disorganization and environmental enforcement in each of these areas to illustrate the relevance of the ToP and political economic analysis for green criminology.

Coal extraction and mountaintop removal

Extracting coal was not always as environmentally destructive as it is now. To reduce the costs of extracting coal and promote the growth of coal as fuel, the coal extraction process has been made "more efficient." By efficient, we mean to capture the coal industry's view – that certain methods of production are cheaper to use, produce more coal, and have a lower unit of production cost. These new methods of withdrawing coal involve open pit mining, strip mining and mountaintop removal mining, which have significantly different environmental impacts from underground mining. In withdrawing coal from the environment through any of these methods, the ToP creates extensive ecological disorganization. How and why?

First, the extraction of coal from the earth requires energy inputs that contribute to ecological disorganization through their withdrawal and use. Second, coal withdrawal techniques result in the physical destruction of the environment. In that process, nature is harmed, often in ways that cannot be repaired, including: the destruction of natural habitat and the disruption of life conditions for natural species; the disruption of water systems including streams and rivers; in some cases, the destruction of an entire ecosystem; and the production of toxic pollutants or mining wastes that impact the quality of the local environment. The ecological disruption associated with coal mining can also impact nutrient flows, lead to the build-up of carbon and/or nitrogen, which may decrease future vegetation growth, and contribute to social problems such as flooding, low levels of natural water recycling, and climate change. Coal withdrawal harms are not limited to the local area where extraction takes place. These methods of withdrawal contribute to deforestation and enhance climate change; they produce toxic waste that harms both human and non-human species in far-off locations once released (e.g., Nriagu 1990).

Mountaintop removal mining is a highly destructive practice in which the tops of mountains are blown up to reveal the coal seam. Many internet websites contain descriptions and photographs of the destruction this process causes. To prepare the mountaintop for mining, trees and soil are removed by large bulldozers. Using this method, the mountaintop ecosystem is essentially pushed off the side of the mountain into adjacent valleys, producing valley fills that block the streams that flow together to create rivers. Thus, not only is the mountaintop's ecosystem destroyed, that destruction contributes to more expansive ecological harms and disorganization. Once the mountain is leveled and the valleys filled, rainwater must find new paths, often leading to localized flooding.

Ecological disorganization caused by current methods of coal extraction is extensive, but is not criminalized to any great extent because coal continues to be the major energy source for most of the world (Ghosh and Prelas 2009), and hence plays a significant role in the treadmill of production. For example, as Ghosh and Prelas (2009) note, coal provides nearly 24.4 per cent of global energy demand and 40.1 per cent of the world's electricity. Globally its use continues to increase (Freese 2003). Much of this increase is driven by China, where coal production accounts for nearly 39.4 per cent of the global total (Ghosh and Prelas 2009: 161–2). Nevertheless, coal production is projected to rise and coal use will increase at a rate of 2.6 per cent growth, and "in 2030, the international coal market will be 44% greater than in 2005" (Editorial Board 2008: 110). This is problematic to the extent that the ecological withdrawal of coal facilitates ecological disorganization. Below, we describe these effects in different coal mining methods.

Underground mining

There are different methods of underground mining. Each method produces environmental harms that have important impacts on environmental quality and stability. Underground mining creates a variety of ecological problems, such as water resource destruction, soil erosion, air and land pollution, the destruction of ecological systems, declining biodiversity, and impairment of health. As Meng *et al.* (2009: 1280) report: "[t]hose problems can interact with each other, and develop through time and space, which speed up the environmental deterioration of coal mining area" [sic]. For example, as mining occurs, so does soil erosion, which is impacted by the physical reshaping of the environment through withdrawal techniques. This physical reconstruction of the environment not only impacts soil and water quality, it can disrupt the natural flow of water systems. Mining activities also generate "acid mine drainage" (Elberling *et al.* 2007), which further impairs water quality. In addition, mining unearths heavy metals such as mercury, lead, zinc, and cadmium, that also enter the local environment, and may drain into local and distant waterways, producing "an instant threat to the biota and the ecological balance by a number of direct and indirect pathways" (Elberling *et al.* 2007). As an example, in parts of China, underground coal mining has completely changed the landscape. One of the problems relates to the use of water resources in mining activities. In some mining techniques, water is employed for extracting and cleaning coal on site. In some areas of China, such large quantities of water have been removed from mining sites that the land above underground water supplies collapses.

Worldwide, there are numerous examples of the negative impacts of underground mining. In the Ukraine, the flooding of mines has contaminated public drinking water (Mokhov 2011). These waters are reported to be high in salinity and contain high sulfate and iron levels (Mokhov 2011; on South Africa see Akcil and Koldas 2006; on Spain, Nieto *et al.* 2007; on Iran, Shahabpour *et al.* 2005). These kinds of mining activities can produce large-scale disasters, the most well known of which is the Buffalo Creek mining disaster in West Virginia in 1972. In the Buffalo Creek disaster 132 million gallons of mining waste was released following heavy rainfall, creating a toxic flood. The floodwaters swept through Buffalo Hollow Creek, killing

126, injuring 1,121, and leaving 4,000 people in a population of about 5,000 homeless (Erikson 1978).

Underground mining is an extremely dangerous activity, and despite its dangers, workers involved in that activity are not well protected by laws or by the companies for which they work (Stickler 2012). The weak nature of underground mining regulations favors the economic interests of the ToP, and illustrates that even the cost of human lives does not slow the withdrawal of natural resources set in motion by the ToP. While mining deaths have declined significantly in the US over time, not all the decline in death is due to criminal, civil, or administrative law; it is also due to the replacement of miners with machinery to facilitate greater levels of production. Machines replace miners because it lowers the cost of production, not because machines make mining safer. For example, if safety were a concern, the condition of mining equipment at the Upper Big Branch Mine, which contributed to the 2010 underground explosion, the largest mining disaster in the US since 1970, would have been maintained more carefully (Stickler 2012). On average over the past several years, data from the US Department of Labor indicates that about 20 miners die in the US each year, and about 3,550 are injured. There are about 86,000 miners in the US. Statistically, the death rate for miners is 22.7 per 100,000, which is four times higher than the homicide rate in the US. In addition, the rate of mining injuries is 4,128 per 100,000 miners, or 16 times higher than the national assault rate. In China, where safety conditions are worse, it is officially reported that as many as 4,700 miners have died annually in recent years. Reviewing these conditions, Wright (2004) argues that it is the economic structure of coal mining in China that leads to violations of safety laws. Mines are located in rural areas, where, due to the transformation in the economy of China, they have become perhaps the only industrial method by which local rural populations can earn a living. In the context of treadmill theory, we can say that the extraction of coal has become increasingly important to the expansion of China's industrial economy. As Wright argues, currently, rural people have little choice but to risk their lives in unsafe mining conditions to earn a living. Essentially, we suggest that these extraction workers are consumed as part of the treadmill withdrawal process, and that the economic efficiency of extraction will remain more important than safety in any system driven to expand the extraction of raw materials in order to push the treadmill forward in its quest for profit.

One of the detrimental outcomes of coal mining that joins worker safety, public health, and ecological destruction together is the threat of underground coal fires produced by ToP withdrawal practices. As Stracher and Taylor (2004: 7) observe:

> Environmentally catastrophic effects from coal fires include the emission of noxious gases and particulate matter into the atmosphere and condensation products responsible for stream and soil pollution. Coal fires have killed people, forced entire communities to abandon their homes and businesses, destroyed floral and faunal habitats, and are responsible for perilous land subsidence.

It has been noted that underground coal fires may burn for years, or even for centuries (Stracher and Taylor 2004). Thousands of coal fires burn constantly throughout the world (Kuenzer *et al.* 2007). These fires pose threats to workers, the public, and the environment. For example, coal fires release significant amounts of mercury and carbon into the environment, and threaten underground water sources. In China, coal fires are estimated to consume approximately 200 million tons of coal per year and contribute about 40 tons of mercury to the environment (Cray 2010; Krajick 2005). These fires may account for as much as 2 to 3 per cent of the annual world emissions of atmospheric carbon dioxide (Stracher and Taylor 2004). In the United States coal fires are also burning out of control. In Pennsylvania, for example, there are well over 100 underground coal fires (Stracher and Taylor 2004). As Stracher and Taylor (2004: 12) note, these fires have likely "contributed to making Pennsylvania the leading acid rain producing state in the U.S." These fires "are responsible for environmental degradation and human suffering. Noxious vapors and toxic fly ash that pollute air, water, and soil promote human disease, including lung and skin cancer as well as asthma and chronic bronchitis" (Stracher and Taylor 2004: 13).

Surface mining

Surface coal mining is a form of coal extraction that takes place above ground. The process involves removing dirt and rocks that cover the coal (called overburden) so that the coal can be extracted from the surface with heavy equipment. In some instances large equipment called draglines, which may be as tall as 220 feet, move massive amounts of earth to get at the coal. In some cases chemical explosives are used to move earth. This type of mining is efficient and consistent with treadmill policies. Surface strip mining is more than two and one-half times as productive as underground mining (US Energy Information Administration 2006). Thus, while the damage done to the ecosystem under strip mining is much more significant than with underground mining, the efficiency of extraction has led to a decline in the price of coal, from $47.77 per short ton in 1978 to $16.84 in 2003. In recent years, however, the price of coal has escalated rapidly, with current prices around $60/ton. The need for energy sources has led to a significant increase in the use of strip mining over the past 30 years, and a significant increase in the global production of coal (from 824 to 1,089 million short tons between 1980 and 2010 in the United States alone, and 683 to 3,829 million short tons in China; US Energy Information Administration 2006).

As an extraction method, strip mining is extremely destructive to the basic ecology of an area (Reece 2006), and it can completely obliterate it. Research indicates that mountaintop removal, which is a type of strip mining, is especially harmful and the overburden (i.e., mountaintops) that are pushed into adjacent valleys can adversely impact water flow and quality (Parker 2007; Reece 2006). Goodell (2006) estimates that mountaintop removal has filled 1,200 miles of streams and headwaters in the United States alone, where there are laws designed to prevent water contamination. Other research indicates that strip mining causes soil erosion, flooding, and a decline in the concentration of important micro-organisms (Pond *et al.* 2008); in short, coal extraction using surface mining techniques is damagingly disruptive to the environment.

Legal controls over strip mining were enacted in the United States in the early 1970s. Since then, the increased use of strip mining has generated considerable attention, yet production has not decreased, as suggested in Figure 3.1. In particular, concerns over the type of strip mining called mountaintop removal have intensified, leading to the formation of several grassroots organizations that oppose the practices and regulations have been created. For example, the Surface Mining Control and Reclamation Act ([SMCRA] Public Law 95-87, created in 1977) was created to "minimize so far as practicable the adverse social, economic, and environmental effects of such mining operations" (30 U.S.C. 1201, Sec. 1201-e). SMCRA also established a fund to help reclaim and restore land and water damaged by past strip mining.

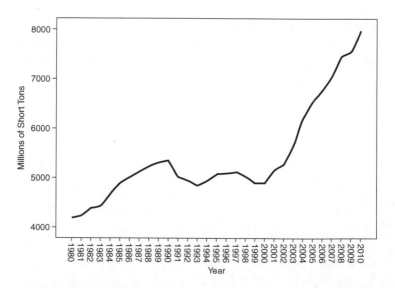

FIGURE 3.1 Global coal production in millions of short tons, 1980–2010
Source: US Energy Information Administration (2012b)

In the United States the Clean Water Act (CWA) regulates coal strip mining when it impacts waterways. The purpose of the CWA is to "restore and maintain the chemical, physical, and biological integrity of the Nation's waters" (Myers *et al.* 2007: 5). Specifically, Section 301 of the CWA makes it a violation (except when done in compliance with the Act) to discharge pollution (including dirt, sand, and stone) into navigable waters – though exceptions are made when discharge and dredge and fill permits are granted (Fuschino 2007).

The coal companies argue that they should be allowed to engage in self-policing of these regulations, and have worked hard to shape environmental regulations and laws that would define ecosystem destruction as illegal, as treadmill theory would suggest. In terms of treadmill actors, coal companies spend considerable sums lobbying the state. For instance, in 2008, the top five US coal mining companies spent $9.95 million lobbying Washington to put pressure on regulatory agencies to alter permit requirements and also to pass legislation favorable to the industry. That year, coal's newest lobbying/ public relations group, the American Coalition for Clean Coal Energy, operated on a $45 million dollar annual budget (Lavelle 2009). After encountering resistance to "clean coal" technology claims at state level, especially in the northeast where states formed coalitions to regulate carbon dioxide emissions from public utilities, coal shifted its political focus to federal level public policy (Lavelle 2009). In short, and consistent with the treadmill of production and the social construction of crime, the coal industry has made noteworthy financial investments to shape the definition of environmental crime, law, and deviance, though it has not done so without local opposition, as will be explored when we discuss social movements. Thus, government interests in coal mining have been shaped by financial interests as the government acts as a mediator of public–private interest conflicts. The state has been unable to balance the interests that lead to these conflicts (O'Connor 1973) and the treadmill dictates that in the end energy policy will win out over environmental protection (Boyce 2002).

Coal's financial strength, coupled with elevated levels of poverty in coal-mining locations, increases the likelihood that coal ToP interests supersede citizen organizations' interest concerning ecological disorganization. This type of environmental injustice is well documented by treadmill theorists (e.g., Gould *et al.* 2008). Treadmill researchers, however, have not examined the role the criminal law might play in addressing this form of ecological disorganization. For example, US federal inspectors report that they have been told to ignore serious environmental problems at large mines and not to issue citations (Parker 1995). The Office of Surface Mining has been accused of failing to make sure that operators pay adequate bonds to reclaim land at large mining operations. Even citizen complaints related to mountaintop blasting, which are considered events that should trigger inspections, have been dismissed in coal-producing states.

Long *et al.* (2012) examined the empirical relationship between coal extraction, environmental violations, and political donations, and hypothesize that donations shape enforcement because companies use their economic power to reject criminal labels that may result from the coal extraction processes. Long *et al.* (2012) discovered that the odds of an environmental violation increased by a factor of 6.25 with each $100,000 donation. Since these donations occurred just *prior* to the discovery of the violation, political donations appear to comprise an effort to alter future enforcement efforts. Treadmill theory supports a political economic interpretation of the operation of law (Chambliss and Seidman 1982), including environmental law (Boyce 2002), indicating that industry's economic interests may supersede ecological destruction and help facilitate ecological disorganization. In the end, a green criminological perspective suggests that state decision-making on coal-mining issues will tend to favor the well-financed and organized coal industry over the local communities where operations exist.

Oil extraction

Oil is a major source of energy in the world. Petroleum makes up nearly 40 per cent of US energy consumption and powers nearly all vehicles. Oil is also used in production to create many industrial chemicals. The history of oil is long and can be traced back nearly

1,000 years. However, the rapid expansion of oil production did not occur until the early 1900s (Maugeri 2006). As Maugeri (2006: 19) notes, at the turn of the century "at least 200 crude by-products had entered daily use, ranging from lubricants for industrial machinery and petroleum wax for pharmaceuticals and candles, to medicines, solvents, and fuel for stoves and internal combustion engines." Energy stored in oil is converted to energy through combustion, which releases carbon into the air and is a major source of climate change, as noted in the next chapter. Since the discovery of efficient oil extraction methods, its production has increased considerably. In fact, the discovery of crude oil led to a significant decrease in the slaughter of whales for oil (Maugeri 2006), allowing whale populations to recover. We discuss the issue of animal production in greater detail later in this book.

Edwin Drake successfully extracted oil from the Pennsylvania earth in 1859. Starting in the 1860s, approximately 1,000 barrels of oil were extracted in the United States daily. By the time oil production reached its peak in the US in 1970, over 9 million barrels of crude oil were produced daily in the United States (US Energy Information Administration 2012a). Today, oil makes up 32.4 per cent of the world's primary energy supply (International Energy Agency 2012). While some scientists believe that global peak oil (the point at which oil production will begin to decline because of supply limits) may be approaching quickly, the production of oil continues to increase at an alarming rate. Most of that production is occurring in the Middle East, where the world's largest oil reserves are located (International Energy Agency 2012).

The extraction of oil is important to green criminology in two ways that relate to the ToP. First, like other withdrawals, the extraction of oil is harmful to ecosystems and their primary production units. Examining these harms expands the concept of crime, and allows criminologists to attend to whether ecological withdrawals are harms deserving legal intervention. Second, oil production and the withdrawal of oil from the environment may be related to social violence. In many instances, crimes are associated with these extractions, and the disruption caused by oil production creates considerable harm that should be labeled as criminal.

Oil drilling can have detrimental, perhaps fatal, effects on the ecosystem. It can contribute to ecological disorganization by harming the ecosystem, including primary production units in an ecosystem. For example, the extraction of petroleum results in oil leaks and other conditions that threaten aquatic systems and biodiversity (Couceiro *et al.* 2010). Moreover, there is increasing empirical evidence that, when petroleum is extracted in forest ecosystems, it acts as a toxin that slows the growth of fungi that form a symbiotic relationship (called mycorrhizal relationship) with forest vegetation roots. This interaction is thought to be extremely important to forest ecosystem development and may actually serve as an interface between forest decomposition and primary ecological production in a way that stimulates growth and prevents plant decease (Robertson *et al.* 2007).

Recently, the quest for oil has lead to the production of oil through the removal of near-surface oil deposits (sand tars and shale-oil). These forms of oil extraction do more than simply damage an ecosystem – they completely obliterate it. The oil-sands extraction processes are similar to surface coal mining, where the overburden is scraped away and the oil-rich sands are collected and processed to extract oil. It takes nearly two tons of sand tar to produce one barrel of oil. Researchers note that the production of oil in this way takes large quantities of land, and destroys ecosystems beyond any possibility for restoration (Johnson and Miyanishi 2008: 122).

The volume of oil extraction has left ecological threats scattered across the global landscape. In Texas, for instance, estimates suggest that nearly one million oil and gas wells were drilled to facilitate oil extraction. As noted, these wells significantly threaten the environment, including water supplies. Examining inactive wells, Merem *et al.* (2010) found that nearly 14,500 inactive wells in Texas are in non-compliance with the law.

The extraction of oil is problematic because, like timber, it leads to forms of state crime. We discuss issues related to social disorganization in later chapters, but point out that conflict arises over oil extraction and use.

Natural gas extraction

A number of the points made in previous sections can be reinforced by examining the practice of hydraulic fracturing. Hydraulic fracturing, or fracking, is a fossil fuel extraction technique used in both oil and, especially, natural gas extraction, that employs a high-pressured chemical mixture of water and solids being injected into dry wells to create seams in shale deposits, to enhance the economic feasibility of fuel recovery. The seams created in shale deposits allow for increased recovery of natural gas from a single well by expanding the reach of the well through the fracturing of underground shale formations.

Fracking is an excellent example of the ToP in action. It involves a treadmill practice invented in 1947 and patented in 1949 by Halliburton (Montgomery and Smith 2010). The development of fracking technology is consistent with Schnaiberg's contentions about the expansion of the ToP in the post-WWII period. Fracking is most widely used in the US and Canada, where 80 per cent of hydrofracturing in the world occurs (Beckwith 2010). Other nations have placed limits on the use of fracking in order to limit its environmental and health consequences.

Significant controversy surrounds fracking. That controversy continues at the present time, and extant scientific research has yet to establish definitive causal connections between fracking and negative human health outcomes, which are required before the law will act to restrict that practice. As a result, US environmental agencies have taken few steps to control fracking. On the precautionary side, however, there is significant evidence favoring fracking control legislation. These concerns are reviewed below.

Fracking requires the use of large quantities of water. A fracking well may use between 1.5 to 5 million gallons of water (Andrews 2009). Because chemicals are mixed with water to make the fracturing process more efficient and to enhance natural gas recovery, the water employed is highly polluted, and may also be contaminated by the heavy metal deposits that occur in shale deposits. The use of large quantities of water also poses depletion problems for local water supplies (Charman 2010). How big a problem does this present? Consider that there are an estimate 35,000 fracking wells operating in the US currently. It can be estimated that those wells require between 52.5 to 175 billion gallons of water. To put that estimate into perspective, Great Salt Lake in Utah, the largest saltwater lake in the western hemisphere, holds about 5 billion gallons of water. In addition, the process of fracking may produce underground fractures that allow the chemicals used in the fracking process to contaminate underground water supplies, as well as lakes, ponds, and streams.

Extant research shows a connection between fracking and human health problems (Finkel and Law 2011), though none has provided the kind of incontestable evidence that meets scientific standards for establishing causality. This has made law-makers slow to react to the problems presented by fracking.

The shale fractures created by fracking may extend as far as 3,000 feet from a well hole – meaning they may be more than a mile in total length (Andrews *et al.* 2009: 22). As a consequence of these large underground fractures, the structure of underground rock formations may become unstable, and result in earthquakes (Kerr 2012).

Until recently, the chemical composition of fracking fluids was treated as a trade secret, which meant that corporations did not have to inform the government concerning the chemicals they were injecting into the ground. While corporations must now report the contents of injected fracking fluids, they do not have to report the volume of each component of the fracking fluid, making it difficult for the government to determine with any certainty the potential health problems a fracking operation may pose.

Recovered fracking fluids are often stored in lagoons above ground, and in that form of containment present their own environmental health problems. Lagoons may rupture, and heavy rains may cause them to overflow, dispersing pollution into the environment.

One of the chemicals added to fracking fluids is carbon dioxide, which enhances the recovery of natural gas by causing the gas to float on well-water columns. These additional pollutants add to forms of ecological disorganization such as climate change. Other chemicals used in this process, such as carbonic acid, also produce chemicals that contribute to climate change.

This short list of fracking consequences would be sufficient to regulate fracking *if* rule-making was based on the precautionary principle. But because environmental rule-making is not based on that principle, many areas in the US have seen tremendous growth in fracking despite its public and environmental health consequences. That result privileges ToP interests over those of the American public.

Other examples of ecological withdrawals

There are many other examples of ecological destructive practice associated with ecological withdrawals. Here, we comment briefly on a few of these to illustrate other ways in which ToP processes generate ecological disorganization. Each of these processes is central to production.

Lead mining

Lead is a heavy metal with known negative biological effects that can impair the neurological functioning of humans and other species. Lead can cause, among many other outcomes, learning deficits, low IQ, and aggression, as well as physical health problems. There are more than four dozen negative health and behavioral consequences that have been associated with lead exposure in empirical research.

As an example of the negative consequences associated with the ecological withdrawal of lead and zinc, consider the case of Picher, Oklahoma, also referred to as the Tar Creek Superfund Site. The Tar Creek Site occupies 1,188 square miles within Oklahoma, Kansas, and Missouri, an area nearly equivalent in size to the entire state of Rhode Island. The first mining activities began in this area in the 1850s. The mines began to be closed in the 1950s due to their environmental impacts. Following the creation of the Comprehensive Environmental Response, Compensation and Liability Act of 1980, Tar Creek was among the first sites designated as a Superfund site under this Act. The problems created by zinc and lead extraction in the Tar Creek area are extensive, and include groundwater pollution; numerous mine tailing piles; wind-blown contaminants; extensive soil contamination; weakening of building and housing structures by lead and zinc mines (86 per cent of existing structures); high levels of lead exposure among the population (e.g., 34 per cent of children tested positive for lead exposure). Due to these effects, its residents largely abandoned the town and, as of the 2010 Census, only six homes, one business, and 20 residents remained. Along with Gilman, Colorado (ordered to be abandoned by the US EPA in 1984), and Wittenoom, Australia (the site of Australia's most significant environmental disaster, abandoned in 1966), Picher became one of only three towns abandoned due to pollution.

Uranium mining

Uranium mining poses significant environmental concerns related to ecological withdrawal. In order to produce uranium, large quantities of raw materials must first be dug from the ground using open pit and underground mining techniques. To illustrate the extent of the effect of uranium mining on the ecology, about 6 tons of raw materials are required to produce 2.2 pounds of uranium. Uranium is extracted from raw materials through chemical leaching, which adds to the pollution problems caused by uranium extraction. The US EPA maintains data on nearly 15,000 uranium mines in 14 US states. About 75 per cent of those mines are on federal and Native American lands, posing significant health problems for Native Americans (Lynch and Stretesky 2012).

The significant impacts caused by the ecological withdrawal of uranium include the discarded raw materials, which remain radioactive, in tailing piles. These tailing piles remain dangerous for an extremely long period of time since the half-life of uranium is about 4.6 billion years. In addition, the excavation of the raw materials employed to make uranium almost always also produces mining waste contaminated with other radioactive materials, including radon and radium. Both open pit and underground mining may cause contamination to water resources both under and above ground.

During mining, the tailings are kept wet to minimize wind erosion. However, after mines are closed, the remaining tailings become subject to wind erosion. The decay of uranium produces 14 different radioactive isotopes, which are of environmental concern. The health of uranium mine workers is also significantly affected by the withdrawal of uranium.

Gold mining

Today, most gold is produced using open pit mining, an extremely damaging form of ecological withdrawal of resources. The environmental group Earthwatch estimates that it takes 20 tons of raw materials to extract enough gold to make one average gold wedding band. The mined raw materials are treated chemically to extract the gold using sulfuric acid, arsenic, and copper, and large quantities of water. This extraction technique degrades the local water supply, especially if run-off from the processing technique is not well contained.

Another dangerous material that tends to coexist with gold deposits is mercury. In processing the raw materials to produce gold, significant amounts of mercury can be released into the environment. The treated waste from the gold extraction process, like other mining waste, is contained in tailing ponds, and includes high concentrations of harmful contaminants such as arsenic, cyanide, and mercury. These tailings remain toxic for centuries, and the withdrawal of gold therefore has significant long-term ecological consequences.

Conclusions

The ToP produces numerous effects on the environment as a consequence of the forms of ecological withdrawals the treadmill favors. Those extraction practices are designed around the interests of capital, and as a result tend to produce adverse consequences for the ecological system, which to the system of capitalism is nothing but a warehouse of stored resources awaiting exploitation. In this sense, it becomes necessary to explore the harms produced, employing explanatory approaches capable of depicting how political economic interests drive the treadmill of production forward in ways that ignore the harms it produces, and that damage the ecological system in ways that cannot be remedied. In that view, we must be willing to recognize that the ToP in its connection to capitalism is willing to sacrifice the health of the ecological system to withdraw raw materials in economically efficient ways that contribute to the production of wealth and its unequal distribution. In terms of green criminology, this means developing explanations of the ToP that conceptualize ToP harms against the environment as crimes against nature produced by the organizational imperatives of capitalism. One way to explore that issue within the context of green criminology is to more fully incorporate the kind of political economic analysis consistent with ToP theory.

4

CRIMES OF ECOLOGICAL ADDITIONS

As described in Chapter 3, production depends on the extraction of natural resources. Production generates ecological additions that often take the form of pollution, and promotes ecological disorganization. Not all forms of pollution are regulated, however, and of those releases that are, an even smaller proportion are treated as criminal. Nevertheless, a variety of ecological additions are disruptive to ecosystems, and may be toxic, producing a variety of green crimes. The treadmill of production not only produces pollution, it plays a role in determining how the state regulates pollution. For the ToP, ecological additions are often an acceptable consequence of production despite the harms they produce (Hillyard *et al.* 2004; Brulle and Pellow 2006). Using ToP concepts, the goal of this chapter is to explore a green criminological explanation of the form and shape of environmental laws, the distribution of environmental enforcement within and across political units, and how spatial and temporal issues influence social and state reactions to ecological additions.

Ecological additions

Schnaiberg (1980) suggests that together with ecological withdrawals, ecological additions represent the two major interactions between the economy and the ecology. Economic production must create pollution because production cannot be perfectly efficient, and as the laws of thermodynamics indicate, production impacts the transformation of matter by generating entropy. Moreover, since capitalism requires continuous economic expansion, it has a tendency to constantly promote the production of ecological additions and entropy. These outcomes are not easily solved by technology, since technological innovations tend to be unable to override the effects of constantly expanding consumption and production linked to capitalism.

Schnaiberg (1980: 27) pointed out that the ecological disorganization created by pollution is a function of several important factors. First, the size of the addition is important. The transition to capitalism, and within capitalism toward a ToP that is chemically and energy intensive, accelerates the release of ecological additions into ecosystems. As demonstrated in previous chapters, environmental additions are clearly increasing in a treadmill fashion. Some of these additions are permanent, accumulate in the environment, and impact food chains, reproduction, and the health of ecosystems, humans, and animals. Schnaiberg (1980: 28) recognized that "modern pollutants tend to have far longer transition times in the atmosphere and in the food chain and nutrient systems of the biosphere." More recently, Colborn, Dumanoski, and Myers (1996) examined hundreds of scientific studies that explore the impact of one kind of ecological addition – endocrine disruptors – on species' reproduction. The researchers proposed that many of the chemicals emitted into the environment interfere with the ecology in a way that alters the sexual development of organisms. In some instances, these additions accumulate and are passed down through generations of organisms. Colborn *et al.* (1996) make a strong case that this form of ecological disruption is increasing over time, as ecological additions accumulate in the environment and because additions have increased significantly as a result of the chemical revolution. From a green criminological perspective, there is reason to believe that environmental law will fail to address this problem efficiently, given the power of treadmill actors and the importance to the expansion of the ToP of the forms of production that produce endocrine disruptors.

Second, as we discuss in this chapter, ecological additions have become increasingly harmful over time as they become more central to expanding economic production (Schnaiberg 1980). The disruptions caused by ecological additions now have global impacts. This point is illustrated in a shift in thinking about planetary history. For example, ecologists Crutzen and Stoermer (2000) have formally proposed that the earth has entered the "anthropocene" era, and that the history of the earth should be described in a way to better reflect how humans impact the world around them. The adoption of the term "anthropocene" within ecology suggests that the current phase of the earth's history must be described in relation to the enormous impact humans have on the ecological system. Sociologists such as Foster, Clark, and York (2010: 14) draw upon this idea of an anthropocene era to argue that an "ecological rift" is developing and threatening the nine planetary boundaries (see Cornell 2012 for a description of these boundaries). These planetary boundaries are "crucial to maintaining an earth-system environment in which humanity can exist safely" (Foster et al. 2010: 14), and the planet's entire ecosystem is in peril if current economic behavior is not modified and pollution trends are not reversed.

With respect to green criminology, it is important to examine why some ecological additions become criminalized while others do not. Ecological additions are inclined to be tolerated when they are central to capitalist production. As production methods change and some chemicals become less important, they are more likely to become regulated. Thus, revealing the relationship between economic centrality and the definition of ecological harm may be an important step in controlling the trends that Schnaiberg identified with respect to increasing chemical pollution over time. In order to consider the issue of ecological additions in detail, we explore the notion of harm that has recently developed in criminology.

Toward the study of ecological additions as green crime

René Truhaut defined ecotoxicology in 1969 as "the branch of toxicology concerned with the study of toxic effects, caused by natural or synthetic pollutants, to the constituents of ecosystems, animal (including human), vegetable and microbial, in an integral context"

(Truhaut 1977: 151). Truhaut proposed that ecosystems should be treated as organisms so that the effects of chemical pollutants could be observed and studied. In general, the key concern among eco-toxicologists today is the effect of pollutants and environmental contaminants on ecosystems and the organisms that inhabit them. The study of ecotoxicology may sometimes include humans as affected organisms, though the study of pollution in ecological systems and its effect on humans is often isolated and treated as environmental toxicology (Walker *et al.* 2006; Zakrzewski 2002). Unfortunately there is still some confusion among scholars concerning the difference between ecotoxicology and environmental toxicology (Forbes and Forbes 1994). In response, Forbes and Forbes (1994: 6) argue that eco-toxicology's proper focus is on "determining the effects of pollutants on the structure and function of intact ecosystems, communities and assemblages." In our view, green criminologists should examine the objective identification of ecological harms in ecotoxicological studies to determine if scientific knowledge concerning ecological harms is translated into environmental laws that deal with ecological additions.

One important issue that emerges within ecotoxicology and environmental toxicology is the definition of the terms "pollution," "pollutants," and "environmental contaminants". Though often treated as interchangeable concepts, these terms distinguish between important scientific concepts. According to Walker *et al.* (2006: i), pollutants and chemical contaminants are "chemicals that exist at levels judged to be above those that would normally occur in any particular component of the environment." The difference between a pollutant and chemical contaminant, then, is based on the outcome: a pollutant is a chemical that causes actual environmental harm; a contaminant is one that does not produce harm. Thus, we adopt the term pollution to describe ecological additions that result in harm to ecosystems and their components.

The harm perspective in criminology

To better advance the notion of green criminology we must address the issue of harm and make it relevant to ecological additions.

Green criminologists were not the first to be concerned with identifying social harms. For example, as Hillyard and Tombs (2007: 18) argue:

> Perhaps the greatest benefit of an analysis of harm is that it would be the basis for developing a much more accurate picture of what is most likely to affect people during their life cycle ... While crime is charted temporally and, increasingly spatially, it is seldom compared with other harmful events ... *a stress upon social harm would also facilitate a focus upon harms caused by chronic conditions or states of affairs – such as exposure to airborne pollutants or to various health hazards at work, poor diet, inadequate housing, unemployment, and so on – as opposed to the discrete events which tend to provide the remit of criminology and the criminal law*. All of these foci would be of benefit for individuals, but they could also provide a basis for more rational social policy. (emphasis added)

Within their concept of harm, Hillyard and Tombs (2007) suggest that the social harm approach would encompass physical harms that involve death or serious injury. Many environmental additions clearly fall within the definition of harm both directly and indirectly and include environmental disasters and ecological disruption and could therefore be defined as green crime. Thus, a harms perspective is shaped by shared understandings and scientific knowledge about what constitutes ecological harm, rather than being a socially constructed concept defined by politicians, as in orthodox criminology. This concept of harm also suggests that power relations tend to influence the structure and content of law, and that this point requires attention from green criminology. For example, anti-toxins activist Lois Gibbs (1997), commenting on pollution-permitting systems used to regulate pollution, remarks that laws governing pollution are simply a "license to kill." She believes that the permitting process is one where corporations are given permission by the government to release toxic chemicals during the production process as long as those releases conform to standards that comply with best technology and cause a relatively low rate of death and illness (e.g., one death per million exposures). Environmental laws are constructed in this way to allow the expansion of production, and to facilitate the economic interests of large producers. As a result, environmental laws make a trade-off between public and environmental health, and economic development and expansion. In this sense, the notion of the kinds of social harm the law represents becomes a contested process with various interest groups (treadmill owners, the state, the public, and scientists) taking different sides in the contest (e.g., Brown *et al.* 2004). While it is difficult to determine which harms might be classified as social harms, green criminology can rely on science for its assessment. Indeed, green criminologists have examined scientific literature to review the harms committed by corporations through the production, distribution, storage, and disposal of pollution that disrupts the ecosystem (Pearce and Tombs 1998; Lynch and Stretesky 2001).

Orthodox criminology generally accepts the criminal law as an appropriate definition of crime. The forces that shape the criminal law, however, lack objective content, and there is significant variation in the criminal law even across US states. In their argument favoring a scientific standard for harm within green criminology over the legal definition of crime preferred by orthodox criminology, Lynch and Stretesky (2001) draw attention to three issues. First, when examining crimes of ecological additions, criminologists can employ medical evidence to identify toxic harms excluded from orthodox measures of crime (e.g., the Uniform Crime Reports or the NCVS). Second, the scope of environmental additions must be placed in context by comparing these harms to the scope of street crimes. As an example, Lynch and Stretesky point to Montague's (1996) comparison of harms produced by assault rifles and pesticides. Montague notes that while assault rifles were associated with an esti-mated 250 homicides in the US in 1995, pesticides killed nearly 10,400 during the same period. Congress, however, is reluctant to discuss legislation that seriously restricts pesticides because, as discussed below, agricultural production is central to chemical manufacturing. Thus, the failure to stop pesticide use is ongoing, while considerable attention and debate is directed toward assault rifles.

Third, Lynch and Stretesky (2001) note that researchers should examine evidence that corporations, at a minimum, are indifferent to the harms their products create. This evidence may be difficult to obtain because corporations often employ elaborate mechanisms to conceal harm (Stauber and Rampton 1995). Nevertheless, many social scientists have shown that products and practices cause harm and that companies are aware of that harm (Fagin and Lavelle 1996; Gibbs 1995; Glantz *et al.* 1998; Karliner 1998; Markowitz and Rosner 2003; Rosner and Markowitz 2007). Green criminologists can examine this harm with respect to ecological additions, noting how specific mechanisms influence state definitions of and enforcement of environmental law, and even the orthodox criminological definition of crime.

Laws governing ecological additions

There are various laws governing ecological additions across the globe. In the United States alone, the number of laws governing ecological additions is impressive and includes many federal protection statutes. One of the earliest attempts to deal with pollution was the Rivers and Harbors Act (RHA) of 1889 (Franz 2010: 255), which prohibits

> throwing, discharging, or depositing any refuse matter of any kind or description from any ship, barge, or floating craft, or from any shore, wharf, manufacturing establishment, or mill into the navigable waters of the United States or their tributaries or onto banks of any such waters where the refuse shall be liable to be washed into such waters, by ordinary or high tides, storms, floods, or otherwise without a permit, or in violation.

One characteristic of this Act is its strict liability nature. Thus, a violation of the RHA does not require a guilty mind. Yeager (1993) has argued that one of the reasons the RHA was created was to facilitate safe navigation of boats in waters. From a ToP perspective, the RHA may not have been passed if it threatened (rather than supported) production. The Act also had a "bounty-hunter" type incentive that allowed individuals who turned in polluters to receive a portion of the fines (Franz 2010). This bounty incentive was and is still used by some environmental groups to control pollution in streams, lakes, and rivers. As will be discussed in Chapter 7, citizen organizations like the Hudson Riverkeepers have used the RHA to help bring suits against river polluters (Cronin and Kennedy 1999).

The Rivers and Harbors Act was a problem for industrial production since most companies rely on externalizing costs of pollution created by releasing pollution into the environment as allowed, for example, under environmental pollution permit systems. As Franz (2010: 263) observes, "into the early 1970s, federal prosecutors continued to bring charges under the RHA ... [and] ... discharges of toxics such as cyanide, phenols, sulfites, and ammonia were found to violate criminal provisions of the RHA." Moreover, the Act was determined to extend to liquid waste and other foreign substances such as petroleum (Franz 2010). Thus, under the RHA, any discharge into the water by a person or corporation could be treated as criminal. According to Franz, using the RHA in this way could significantly impact production since more than 99 percent of the estimated 40,000 industrial production plants in the US were subject to criminal indictments. Moreover, the bounty hunter clause made detection and prosecution likely. While industry challenged the RHA in court to get exceptions to the Act, in 1970 the US created the Environmental Protection Agency and began issuing permits to release water pollution under the Federal Water Pollution Control Act (FWPCA) of 1972. Franz (2010: 266) argues that the FWPCA helped protect industries by allowing pollution to be expelled into waterways under pollution permit systems, ending the influence of the RHA as a mechanism for controlling ecological additions to waterways. Figure 4.1 shows the drop in RHA cases after the creation of the FWPCA. The demise of the RHA shows how environmental laws have been influenced by production practices. Laws that threaten production by limiting emissions are opposed by industry, which shapes both laws and ecological additions.

The chemical revolution transformed pollution regulation, and gave rise to an elaborate civil and administrative system of control. In the US, the Resource Conservation and Recovery Act, the Clean

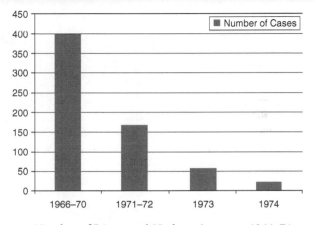

FIGURE 4.1 Number of Rivers and Harbors Act cases, 1966–74
Source: Based on data in Franz (2010)

Water Act, the Comprehensive Environmental Response, Compensation and Liability Act, the Federal Insecticide, Fungicide and Rodenticide Act, the Toxic Substances Control Act, and the Safe Drinking Water Act, comprise a significant portion of pollution regulations. These laws are primarily enforced through civil administrative actions taken by the Environmental Protection Agency or state agencies. This means that the majority of violations do not invoke the judicial process (Burns *et al.* 2008). Instead, environmental enforcement largely relies on organizational actions within the Environmental Protection Agency, including notices of violation and administrative orders that ask companies to comply with the law or pay a small penalty for violating an Act. Formal civil and criminal cases are uncommon and number in the low hundreds annually. More serious infractions are typically filed with the US Department of Justice or by a state agency on behalf of the EPA (Burns *et al.* 2008). A small number of environmental offenders receive prison sentences or large fines, and these are typically publicized by the EPA and used to help demonstrate that the agency is protecting the environment. Few criminal environmental crime cases are pursued by the federal government. For example, in 2011, the US EPA listed 24 completed criminal case convictions (begun in various years) involving 20 federal Acts and all 50 states (to access these criminal data, see http://cfpub.epa.gov/compliance/criminal_prosecution/).

While the government attempts to use civil and administrative law to regulate environmental harms and protect public and environmental health, environmental protection is often shaped by grassroots political activism (Bullard 1993; Gibbs 1995) and moral crusades (Friedrichs 1996: 17–19). As a mechanism of social control, environmental law does little to slow down the treadmill's ecologically destructive consequences (Stretesky *et al.* 2012).

The role of corporate and state actors

Chapter 2 reviewed the four key actors that play a role in maintaining the ToP. In the case of ecological additions, the state and corporations often act together to maintain ecological additions. As noted, the state issues permits that allow corporations to emit toxins and pollutants into the environment. In many instances the government ignores or misrepresents the harmful effects of toxic waste (Fagin and Lavelle 1996; Karliner 1998), or pursues policies that allow industry to regulate itself (Stretesky 2006). This occurs for a number of reasons but, as previously suggested, the state tends not to act in ways that reduce the negative ecological impacts of corporations and the production of ecological disorganization. In this sense, the state facilitates green harms caused by corporations. For green criminology, this opens up the possibility of examining these kinds of acts as state-corporate crimes (Lynch *et al.* 2010). The concept of state-corporate crime developed by Michalowski and Kramer (2007) can contribute to a green criminological analysis of how the ToP helps produce ecological disorganization (Kramer and Michalowski 2012; Kramer 2012). Michalowski and Kramer point out that corporate crime can take two forms. One form is initiated by the state and the other is facilitated by the state. The notion of state-facilitated corporate crime is most consistent with ToP theory and Schnaiberg's (1980) work, because it exists when the governmental regulatory system fails to prevent ecological disorganization that results from increasing production.

This occurs, according to Michalowski and Kramer, because corporations and the government share similar goals and because the state would like to gain revenue to advance neo-liberal practices that expand tax revenues.

Also important to the concept of state-corporate crime is the notion of harm that encompasses criminal, regulatory, and other destructive practices. As Michalowski and Kramer (2007: 202) argue, the distinction between "crime and regulatory violations is itself an expression of political power ... that can only be caused by corporate and governmental elites [in a] juridical move prompted by the interests of the same economic and political elites it was designed to control." The criminological notion of harm in state-corporate crime is consistent with the notion of ecological disorganization described by Schnaiberg (1980).

State agencies may misrepresent the harmful effects of toxin exposure, leading to a lack of protective legislation. Consequently, it is necessary to assess questions of harm independently of definitions of environmental crime provided by law. As an example of how the concept of state-corporate crime relates to ToP, consider the issue of self-policing. Self-policing occurs when a company is offered an economic incentive, such as reduced penalties, to report its administrative, civil, and criminal violations to the proper state authorities. The idea that self-policing can prevent crime is becoming increasingly popular among policy-makers (Freeman 2000; Stretesky 2007). Trends in environmental self-policing are characteristic of general trends in state-corporate regulatory policy that Michalowski and Kramer (2007) identify as problematic. In our view, the move toward environmental self-policing represents a step away from traditional enforcement and toward forms of cooperation that can ensure the success of the market. Self-policing, then, is a move away from a system of punishment where the state determines the rules and regulations and establishes punishment for administrative, civil, and criminal violations. The move from traditional enforcement to market-based incentives means that corporations increasingly become more connected to the state and influence how they will or will not be regulated.

The shift toward self-regulation began in the early 1990s and changed the nature of environmental regulation dramatically (Kraft and Vig 2000). Specifically, this new environmental policy allows companies to conduct routine production audits without fear that those audits will be used against them. Any harm uncovered during production audits may merely be reported and corrected as a cost of doing business. This shift in forms of regulation in the US not only reinforces but expands the relationship between political and economic interests to protect the ToP.

In global regulation, state-facilitated corporate crime also applies to the concept of the "race to the bottom" (Porter 1999). Specifically, this concept is one where corporations seek out countries with the lowest operating costs. These reduced operating costs come in the form of minimal taxes, wages, and environmental standards and enforcement that may regulate ecological additions. If we accept the idea that an impending ecological crisis will occur if production continues to increase, then the concept of the race to the bottom is applicable to state-facilitated corporate crime. Examples in the criminological literature include the analysis by Pearce and Tombs (1998) of Union Carbide's chemical disaster in Bhopal, India in 1984. The company was able to reduce the costs of environmental regulation by operating a subsidiary chemical facility in India, for reasons of lower operating costs (Pearce and Tombs 1998). The relative lack of safety regulations at the Bhopal facility, combined with the pressure on the facility to create significant profit, are the reasons widely accepted for the toxic release that has now killed an estimated 25,000 people and injured nearly half a million (Post 2012). The ecological damage caused by Bhopal was significant and remains unremediated (Pal and Dutta 2012). Conditions consistent with the Union Carbide Bhopal disaster are played out every day across the globe and many result in significant ecological disorganization (White 2012a). Specifically, allowing corporations to create ecological disorganization in countries because of political instability, economic deprivation, and weak environmental protection is a form of state-facilitated corporate crime. Green criminologists have yet to seriously examine this form of state-facilitated corporate crime (except see Tombs 2012) and the environmental inequality that may emerge as a result. Recent work on environmental justice has been examining the human harms and violence associated with the global move of capital from core to periphery nations (Morales *et al.* 2012). In short, global environmental inequality occurs when environmental benefits and burdens are not fairly distributed across countries, and environmental problems are concentrated in those countries where there is the highest level of poverty and economic disadvantage (Morales *et al.* 2012). Thus, moving production to maximize profit may result in significant ecological damage to the ecosystems because pollution is concentrated in the most impoverished countries.

Corporate actors and environmental enforcement

Notions of harm and state-corporate crime are related to the forms of pollution the law fails to criminalize, since law-making is heavily influenced by corporate interests (Colburn *et al.* 1996; Erhlich and Erhlich 1998; Fagin and Lavelle 1996). Thus, in the long run, industry interests protecting the ToP have held greater sway than those expressed by environmental organizations and research scientists, resulting in laws favoring corporate profit-making over the health of the ecological system. The relationship between ecological additions and the law is an important area of study for green criminology.

According to Schnaiberg (1980), treadmill institutions directly oppose constraints on production. For instance, companies advertise their pursuit of "green production" technology while mobilizing significant resources against any enforcement that may constrain the expansion of production. Gould *et al.* (2008) specifically suggest that treadmill corporations will use their economic power to shape the political landscape. This argument extends to criminal justice and attempts by companies to reject criminal labels by influencing laws or enforcement. As Fagin and Lavelle (1996) have noted, one way to shape the enforcement landscape is to effectively counteract legislation and enforcement practices that may limit production. For corporations, this is accomplished through effective public campaigns, lobbying, and the manipulation of scientific results in the political and public arenas. When production practices are challenged, corporations typically deny any evidence of harm (Fagin and Lavelle 1996). Next, corporate methods of influencing political actors often include claims that proposed regulation is based on inappropriate or inadequate science (or "junk science") and that studies do not adequately model human exposure or ecosystems. Corporations then ask for new studies. Fagin and Lavelle suggest that producers often pay for new studies that can then be used to lobby for a stop to legislation and for public support for production.

At the same time, industry attacks the science that contradicts production; they promote the economic benefit of production to labor and the state. In short, industry is able to manipulate laws through these mechanisms (Beder 2001). As Fagin and Lavelle (1996: 13) argue, "the federal regulatory system is driven by the economic imperatives of the chemical manufacturers – to expand markets and profits." Evidence of lobbying for environmental laws on the part of industry is pervasive in the United States and is growing globally (Beder 2001; Farber 1992; Ydersbond 2011). As Beder (2001: 249) argues, "corporations managed to achieve a virtual moratorium on new environmental legislation in many countries throughout the late 1970s and most of the 1980s," through donations to politicians and lobbying governments.

Gould *et al.* (1996) note that corporate resistance to legislation is often carried out through lobbying and donation practices that ironically reflect the "problematic alliance between corporation and the state ... [and have] implications for environmental protection in particular." The focus on the power of corporations to influence environmental protection through direct and indirect donations and political lobbying suggests that the threat of enforcement against corporations is associated with the level of political donations and lobbying by those corporations in order to manipulate the law and ensure that companies are not treated as criminals for their ecological destruction. Thus, we see environmental enforcement as an organizational outcome that is related to power struggles between civil society, state agencies, producers, and labor (Gould *et al.* 1996).

As noted in Chapter 2, the political economy of production and consumption may also influence the level of enforcement brought to bear on those corporations central to the ToP. When production is central to capitalist expansion, the behavior of actors engaging in that sector is less likely to be criminalized by environmental law, given its economic value to the economic and political elite.

Pollution

Research on ecological additions demonstrates that production-related pollution has a significant impact on ecosystems and the biosphere. For example, in the US alone, 3.337 billion pounds of toxic waste were reportedly released into the environment in 2009 under the Toxic Release Inventory (TRI) program (Lynch *et al.* 2010). However, toxic releases reported in the TRI represent only a small fraction of all production-related releases worldwide. Moreover, the TRI does not record all pollution in the US, since some forms of pollution are unregulated, and because TRI data is self-reported by industries that produce them. However, pollution is a global problem and the damage from pollution is not limited to the ecosystem in which it is created. Air pollution, in the form of brown clouds, moves across continents and ocean basins, causing a dimming effect that reflects sunlight away from the earth, altering weather patterns in certain areas of the globe (Ramanathan and Feng 2009). The effect of these pollution clouds is that ecosystems are changed because it slows the hydrological cycle, discussed in Chapter 1. These brown clouds also have consequences for the biosphere. Pollution has become so ubiquitous that it is found in areas not inhabited by humans, which have no local, industrial sources of pollution (e.g., the Arctic and Antarctic: Camarero *et al.* 2009). Indeed, in some ecosystems and among some groups of individuals, the extent of background pollution (pollution that is already present in an ecosystem or body) is considered so pervasive that it is difficult for scientists to determine whether a particular pollution source is having an undesirable impact (Pujades-Rodriquez *et al.* 2009; Reopanichkul *et al.* 2010; Van der Hoeven 2012).

It is also important to recognize that the ecological destruction caused by production-related pollution is not distributed equally across the globe – though everyone is impacted. The rapid industrialization of China, for instance, has significantly impacted their ecosystem and the health of millions of China's citizens. Khan *et al.* (2008) suggest that the heavy metals associated with industrialization have found their way to agricultural soils and have been taken up by plants in such large quantities that they violate the standards of China's Environmental Protection Agency as well as those set by the World Health Organization. Research in China also indicates that the longest river in Asia, the Yangtze, has been significantly impacted by production-related pollution (Müller *et al.* 2008). Recent reports suggest that billions of pounds of untreated pollution from industrial production are pumped into the Yangtze annually (Economy 2004). Moreover, in one 82-mile stretch of water in the Huai basin, the water is rated by the Chinese government as "too toxic to touch" (Yardley 2004). Chinese citizens have long been subject to high levels of industrial pollution, but have rarely been the subjects of news stories, let alone criminological research examining their plight and circumstances (Economy 2004). The green crimes taking place in Chinese ecosystems are generally ignored by criminologists, and the people's plight as human victims of state-corporate crime goes unnoticed despite the tremendous harm they face.

As the example of China illustrates, the ToP creates ecological disorganization that is global in scope. This occurs because green crime is driven by the fundamental organizational structures of the global economy and its manifestations in individual nations. Green criminologists from around the globe are beginning to examine the connection between green crime and human harm in the context of local and global pollution regulation. Walters (2010: 309; see also Lynch and Stretesky 2001) suggests that criminology is focused too heavily on "physical, psychological and social violence, yet notions of environmental harm and ecological destruction have been conspicuously absent" (Walters 2010: 315). By focusing attention on pollution regulation in several different states, Walters (2010: 320) argues for enhanced global enforcement of ecological additions to minimize ecological, human, and non-human harm. He notes, however, that under the current economic system it is "difficult to envisage a decline in the harms caused by pollution" (Walters 2010: 320). We agree with Walters that without fundamental changes in production, harm to humans and the ecosystems on which we depend will continue.

The legal definition of environmental crime, however, is more likely to preserve the ToP than to challenge the forms of ecological disorganization it creates. This has much to do with the relationship between the interests of the powerful and their influence on environmental law-making. At issue here is the difference between how the law currently responds to environmental harms and how it ought to respond to environmental harm. On this point, what should we make of Walters' (2010) discussion of World Health Organization (WHO) estimates that 2.4 million people around the world die prematurely from exposure to air pollution each year? Is the law the correct way to control this kind of outcome?

To place the WHO estimate in perspective, its figure of 2.4 million premature deaths a year is five times the number of homicides (about 485,000) that occur in the world annually. In addition, this figure of deaths from exposure to air pollution does not include estimates of death related to a now widespread cause of air pollution – global warming. Estimates of deaths due to global warming (examined below) currently stand at 400,000 worldwide annually (DARA, 2012). Thus, there may be as many as 4.3 million deaths due to air pollution in its various forms, a total that is nine times the number of deaths due to homicides around the world. Because climate change and global warming are such pervasive problems, we examine below the ecological additions associated with this particular issue in detail, relating them to notions of harm and green crime.

Global warming

As noted, the destruction of the ecosystem associated with ecological additions in the form of various types of pollution is considerable. Yet, the ecological disorganization caused by pollution, in general, appears insignificant when examined in comparison to the harm caused by a specific type of pollution known as greenhouse gases. Greenhouse gases are chemicals in the atmosphere that trap heat in the earth's atmosphere and contribute to an increase in the earth's temperature (Houghton *et al.* 1996). The trapped heat causes the planet to warm and therefore disorganizes ecosystems and the biosphere significantly by altering the ecosystem's production cycles (see Chapter 1). Scientists have long known about the problem of climate change. In the nineteenth century, James Fourier (1878) discovered that gases in the earth's atmosphere could cause a "greenhouse" effect by absorbing radiant heat, an observation confirmed by John Tyndall (1861) who identified carbon dioxide and water vapor as central to this process. In 1896, these observations allowed the Swedish chemist Savante Arrhenius (1908) to demonstrate how increased levels of atmospheric carbon dioxide could alter the earth's atmospheric temperature. These discoveries, however, had little scientific impact until computer modeling was used in conjunction with advanced measurements of carbon in the atmosphere to provide more conclusive evidence on climate change (Lovelock 2007). The ecological harm associated with climate change has thus been known for some time. Today, the vast majority of scientists agree that human-related production of carbon and other global warming gases is having more of an impact on climate change than any natural cause (Crowley 2000). In short, scientific consensus suggests that contemporary global warming has anthropogenic (human) causes (IPCC 2007). That scientific discovery forms the basis for examining the ecological disorganization caused by climate change.

Because greenhouse gases are related to global warming, the amount of gases released by humans can be modeled to determine how those releases change ecosystems, producing outcomes such as increasing mean global temperature, melting ice caps, and rises in sea level (Meehl *et al.* 2005). The consequences of climate change are being felt worldwide. For instance, thousands of residents who have lived on small islands in the Pacific impacted by climate change have plans to evacuate their homes by the end of the century (Fisher 2011). In 2009, climate change evacuations began in the

Carteret Islands. Rising sea levels and an increased frequency and intensity of storms threatened the fresh-water supplies of some island residents. In the case of Tuvalu, traditional and sustainable agricultural practices have changed because the land is being contaminated by salt-water invasion from storms, floods, and rising sea levels (Lazrus 2010).

Research suggests that increasing levels of carbon dioxide in the atmosphere can alter ecosystems by increasing the emissions of other naturally occurring greenhouse gases, such as nitrous oxide from soils and methane from wetlands (Van Groenigen et al. 2011). This finding has implications for the ability of ecosystems to withstand further carbon dioxide pollution and signals that damage to local ecosystems may impact the biosphere and cause planetary boundaries (i.e., the point of no return) to be reached much more quickly than anticipated (Foster et al. 2010).

Research makes it clear that climate change has impacted nearly every part of the world. Brommer and Møller (2010) suggest that climate change impacts where birds reside within an ecosystem and note that some species of birds may die out as a result. Elsewhere it has been shown that polar bears are among the first animal species to experience extensive loss of habitat and it is estimated that climate change could result in a significantly greater number of polar bear deaths as a result of starvation (Molnár 2010). Climate-induced changes in ecosystems are also observed when examining plants and vegetation (Gottfried et al. 2012; Walther et al. 2009), and fisheries around the world are being impacted by changes in the climate that create stress in fish and reduce their numbers (Allison et al. 2009). As a result of these changes in the ecology, forced by the global economy, many nations will see significant destruction not only to valuable ecological systems within their borders but to human and animal populations. Allison et al. (2009) suggest that a significant proportion of the human population in several countries that depend on fish consumption will die because of the effects of climate change. Even Inupiat Eskimos, inhabiting the village of Shishmaref in Alaska, face evacuation as waves that are normally buffered by sea ice erode the coast and invade their village (Bronen 2009; Marino 2011). In Bangladesh, significant changes to the ecosystem have reduced the volume of crops that can be planted, and thousands of acres of crop-land are lost to rising sea levels and river erosion associated with the melting of the Himalayan glaciers each year. This change alone is thought to impact nearly one million residents (Xu *et al.* 2009).

Global warming is an area where green criminologists are just now beginning to focus a significant amount of attention (Agnew 2011; Kramer and Michalowski 2012; Lynch *et al.* 2010; White 2012a; Kramer 2012). This attention is directed toward damage to the ecosystems, as well as state and corporate connections and emerging global inequality associated with production of ecological harm and the distribution of global-warming gases (White 2012b).

State-corporate connections that facilitate the production of global-warming gases such as carbon dioxide and increase harm are discussed in the green crime literature. Drawing on these connections with respect to climate change, Lynch, Burns, and Stretesky (2010: 220) report that several former energy sector lobbyists and corporate executives held important positions in the cabinet of former President George Bush. These positions included James Connaughton, a former power company lobbyist and Chair of the White House Council on Environmental Quality, and Rebecca Watson, who was a former lawyer for methane drillers and Assistant Secretary for Lands and Mineral Management (Lynch *et al.* 2010). Many of these cabinet members helped push for energy policies that facilitate the treadmill, including drilling for oil in the Arctic. As Lynch *et al.* (2010) document, ToP energy interests have successfully impacted the state, and led the federal government to withdraw existing environmental protection standards that once restricted various segments of the energy sector. This includes rewriting environmental rules that facilitate energy policy when necessary for production, including amendments to the New Source Review (NSR) rules related to air pollution criteria, in order to allow the construction of new coal-based electrical power plants. Other changes to NSR rules include a provision for increased air pollution emissions, including carbon emissions, from "coal fired" power plants.

It should also be noted that there is a significant amount of variation in the production of global-warming gases globally

(Stretesky and Lynch 2009). Over the past three decades there has been a geographic shift in the distribution of global carbon dioxide production. This shift occurred as manufacturing contracted in the US and expanded in countries with low labor costs and/or less restrictive environmental regulations, including China. Thus, the ToP has global consequences for green crime research. Trends in environmental legislation need to be examined globally because, as global commodity chain research suggests, the consumption of energy has increased as goods must be transported from manufacturing and assembly locations in peripheral nations in order to be sold in core nations. The movement of the production and goods to developing nations will likely influence corporate-state connections and produce significant variations in ecological additions and disruptions across countries (Jorgenson 2011; Jorgenson and Clark 2011).

Given this high degree of interdependency, world system theory depicts the economy as a global commodity chain that consists of worldwide networks of labor and production processes (Appelbaum and Christerson 1997). This commodity chain helps to explain the shifts in international production practices over the past 30 years and the reasons why production has moved from wealthy, developed countries to poor, undeveloped countries. Grimes and Kentor (2003: 273) argue that "less developed countries became parts suppliers to the global economy" because many companies now manufacture product components in several different countries and have them shipped to yet another country for assembly. Thus, the inequality in the distribution of global-warming gases that arises because of the need to expand production is considerable, and suggests that, globally, there is an inequality in the creation of environmental regulation that is driven by economic interests, and facilitates production and the expansion of capital (Stretesky and Lynch 2009).

Summary

Production-related pollution is a significant contributor to ecological disorganization and disruption and should be of considerable interest to criminologists. With the exception of green criminology, however, criminologists generally ignore the problem of ecological disorganization as crime.

The study of the forms of ecological disorganization caused by ecological additions has a number of implications for criminology. First, this should draw attention to the interrelationship between economic relations and the definition of environmental crime in the law. As an organizational structure, environmental law tends to facilitate rather than control ecological additions. It does so because powerful treadmill actors use their economic power to shape the law and, in shaping the law, also provide incentives to state agents to protect the ToP through lobbying and campaign contributions.

Second, ecological additions produce environmental injustice, an issue that we have paid significant attention to in our own applications of green criminology (Long *et al.* 2012). Third, the forms of harm produced by ecological additions have implications for green criminologists researching harms against animals. This issue has been underdeveloped in green criminology, and we address this concern in Chapter 6.

Fourth, and perhaps the most significant issue in the study of the ToP, ecological additions and ecological disorganization draw attention to the definition of crime typically employed by criminologists, and especially orthodox criminologists. Orthodox criminology defines crime as a violation of the criminal law, and hence omits the examination of green crimes, since they are not violations of the criminal law as traditionally defined. In redefining crime to include green crime, green criminologists should make use of scientific evidence concerning the harms ecological additions produce in order to illustrate the objective nature of a green criminological definition of crime that is independent from the capricious and subjective content of the criminal law definition of crime.

In the next chapter, we turn our attention to how a political economic view, associated with ToP theory, can be employed to explore crime and violence.

5

ECOLOGICAL AND SOCIAL DISORGANIZATION

Up until this point, we have focused exclusively on explaining the ToP, and the ecological disorganization that is a result of this process. In this chapter, we turn to the association between ecological disorganization and social disorganization. Although an analysis of this link has been neglected, it is important to highlight it in order to demonstrate the widespread social impacts of the treadmill and the influence of the treadmill on traditional crime and violence. This chapter introduces the concept of social disorganization and then moves to a discussion of how ecological and social disorganization are related. The following section discusses how ecological and social disorganization can lead to traditional (non-green) crimes. We conclude by suggesting an agenda for future research that examines both ecological and social organization.

Social disorganization

Social disorganization has been a popular explanation in orthodox criminology for almost 100 years. The theory suggests that urbanization, industrialization, and immigration weaken social bonds and conventional beliefs and values, and lead to higher rates of crime. The social "disorganization" that results from rapid transitions and immigration causes crime to increase.

Arguably the first study of social disorganization was conducted by Thomas and Znaniecki (1919). Their classic study, *The Polish*

Peasant in Europe and America, described the adjustment of Polish rural peasants to life in the urban United States after immigration. The cultural values and beliefs of peasant life did not translate well to city life, and the result was higher rates of crime and delinquency among that population. Sociologists at the University of Chicago used Thomas and Znaniecki's work as they began formulating the study of *human ecology* (Park and Burgess 1984 [1919]), the examination of how people interact and are affected by their environment. People in urban environments are constantly competing for resources (e.g., income and jobs), and are therefore at the mercy of their environment and the other people who live close to them. Park and Burgess attempted to show how Chicago is broken down into "zones", which have decreasing levels of social disorganization and consequently crime, moving from the city center out toward the suburbs.

Human ecology is a useful approach for studying how people adapt to living in a disorganized environment that includes changing cultural norms and values and unequal access to resources, particularly in urban areas. Shaw and McKay (1942), also from the University of Chicago, found that high delinquency rates were a stable, persistent characteristic of the Chicago neighborhoods in which they were observed. These high-crime areas persisted regardless of the ethnicity of the residents of the area, leading Shaw and McKay to conclude that values and beliefs, coupled with their economic position, were the main determinants of crime. Furthermore, "Shaw and McKay argued that three structural factors – low economic status, ethnic heterogeneity and residential mobility – led to the disruption of community social organization, which, in turn, accounted for variations in crime and delinquency" (Sampson and Groves 1989). In sum, the historical arguments of social disorganization theory focus on crime as a typical outcome in urban areas where rapid changes to cultural values and belief systems have occurred. These new value structures lead to anomie, which in turn causes crime rates to increase.

While Shaw and McKay's work was groundbreaking in the theoretical sense, it was difficult for them and subsequent researchers to empirically test hypotheses based on social disorganization. The work of Shaw and McKay was predominantly descriptive, and therefore numerous assumptions had to be made about the causal mechanisms of the social disorganization process. Social disorganization theory should be tested across communities, because it is hypothesizing relationships *between* communities (Sampson and Groves 1989: 776). Sampson and Groves (1989) conducted the first true empirical test of social disorganization theory, in which they analyzed data on 238 localities in Great Britain. They found that structural factors (economic status, ethnic heterogeneity, residential mobility), along with intervening variables (ability of a community to supervise and control teenage peer groups, informal local friendship networks, and rate of local participation in formal and voluntary organizations), significantly predicted social disorganization. Subsequent empirical work has supported the findings of Sampson and Groves (Veysey and Messner 1999), and suggested new directions for social disorganization theory (Kubrin and Weitzer 2003).

Overall, the work on social disorganization posits that crime is the result of the lack (or dissolution) of social bonds and changing cultural values. These processes often happen in time of rapid transitions (industrialization and urbanization) and immigration. However, research has shown that social disorganization occurs regardless of ethnicity, therefore leading scholars to conclude that it is not individual characteristics that lead one to commit crimes; rather, economic status and the anomie that is created by structural factors leads to social disorganization and crime. We believe that the relationship between the economy and the environment represents one set of structural relationships that influence social disorganization, and therefore helps to explain more orthodox forms of crime and delinquency. That is, ecological disorganization influences social disorganization.

Ecological and social disorganization

Social disorganization has been used extensively to explain street crimes in the criminology literature. Yet, the links between ecological disorganization and social disorganization remain uninvestigated. Recall that ecological disorganization occurs when relationships between organisms (plants, animals, etc.) and their environment are altered. As we reviewed in Chapter 2, capitalism is the main cause of ecological disorganization in the contemporary world. Similar to ecological disorganization, social disorganization also examines the relationship between organisms (i.e., humans) and their environment. We argue that it is likely the case that ecological disorganization and destruction to ecosystems may create social disorganization. We extend treadmill theory to suggest that social problems (e.g., unemployment, conflict, crime, and violence) often stem from exploitative relationships between the ecology and the economy, such as the rapid extraction of natural resources, armed conflict over natural resources, and the potential impacts of pollution on humans that weakens social bonds to conventional institutions. In order to elaborate on this point further we examine the links between ecological and social disorganization in more detail.

At first blush an association between these two concepts might not be immediately apparent, because social disorganization is focused exclusively on humans, human transitions, and their built environment, whereas ecological disorganization is a process that unfolds between humans and the natural environment. However, it is our contention that these concepts are linked. In Chapters 3 and 4 we explained the two major categories of green crime: crimes of withdrawal and crimes of addition. Here we discuss a different type of crime: crimes against the working class, crimes against the powerless and marginalized. In the next section we explore the links between ecological and social disorganization with respect to the three major actors in the treadmill: labor, the state, and corporate actors.

Labor

The relationship between ecological and social disorganization is clear in the case of labor. As described in Chapter 2, the labor component of the treadmill is predominantly concerned with job creation and job loss. As capital attempts to accumulate greater and greater amounts of surplus value, labor suffers because unemployment increases (Lynch and Michalowski 2006; Schnaiberg 1980). Technological advances that rely on processes that create ecological disorganization tend to decrease the need for labor and therefore increase social disorganization and destroy ecosystems. Thus, two types of crimes are being generated by capital: crimes against ecosystems (or green crime) and crimes against the working classes that are a result of the social disorganization generated by the relationship between the ecology and economy. Many social commentators have argued that this potential of capitalism to create widespread unemployment, through technology, chemical technology, and biotechnology, represents the end of work and consequently levels of social disorganization that are simply unthinkable and have the potential to destroy or completely reorganize social institutions (Rifkin 1995).

To illustrate this process, we draw upon the information presented in Chapter 3 examining the extraction of natural resources (oil, timber, coal), and in Chapter 4 examining the increasing use of chemicals in production. These two trends are problematic because they are environmentally destructive and socially destructive. In short, the widespread use of chemically intensive extraction and production techniques increases ecological disorganization by introducing toxic chemicals into the environment, and increases social disorganization by decreasing the number of jobs in those extraction and production industries. The impact of unemployment on crime is well studied in the criminological literature. And, while there is strong theoretical reason to believe that unemployment is related to crime that ranges from orthodox to radical explanations (Becker 1968; Cantor and Land 1985; Gordon 1973), there has been some disagreement as to the strength of the empirical relationship. Nevertheless, according to Chiricos (1987) most studies of unemployment and street crime find a positive relationship between the two variables. This uncertainty in the crime–unemployment relationship is likely a result of what Cantor and Land (1985) have described as the counteracting effects of unemployment that include both guardianship – which creates a negative relationship between unemployment and crime – and criminal motivation, which creates a positive relationship between unemployment and crime matter. More recent research into the effects of crime indicates that motivation is the driving force for long-run trends in unemployment and street crime, suggesting that as time wears on the unemployed are more likely to be motivated to commit crime and that this effect can alter the very social fabric of their neighborhoods by creating significant levels of disorganization over time (Andresen 2012). In short, we see the importance of unemployment in the context of treadmill theory where changes in production have facilitated ecological disorganization and social disorganization.

A second example of the link between ecological and social disorganization can be observed in the case of mountaintop removal coal mining. Initially, labor is attracted to the area to work in the mine. Mountaintop mining is a relatively quick process: the mining company blows the top off the mountain to reveal coal seams, the miners strip the coal, and when the coal is gone, the mine shuts down. During the time the mining operation is open, the town where the mine is located experiences an economic boom, with stores to service the miners, and the miners spending money in the town. However, when the mine closes and the primary income source of the miners is no longer available, the locals cease to benefit from the additional revenue brought in by the miners, and social disorganization follows. Some miners and townspeople find themselves unemployed; others may remain employed but see a reduction in their income. Research in criminology has begun to look at the link between natural resource extraction and crime more generally, focusing on how extraction changes the social fabric of an area by disrupting traditional employment and lifestyles. For instance, drawing upon social disorganization theory, Carrington, Hogg, and McIntosh (2011: 353–4) point out that in Australia:

> One of the many costs [of natural resource extraction] may be a rise in violence and other social harms in communities affected by the mining and energy sector. These are seriously under-recognized issues and there remains a paucity of empirical data and conceptual understanding of the criminological impact of post-industrial mining regimes and a lack of policy or regulatory approaches to contend with the problems.

In the United States researchers such as Schwaner and Keil (2003: 280) have found evidence of social disruption in coal counties in the United States, arguing that "coal-producing companies from Pennsylvania, Ohio, and New York utilized cheap labor to mine the coal reserves while transferring capital out of state leaving economic distress." The researchers suggest that within coal-mining counties in Appalachia, violence is often used as an informal form of social control to aid in the extraction of natural resources. These coal-mining counties had higher levels of poverty and unemployment and suffered from serious economic distress.

The state

While not as immediately obvious as the link between ecological and social disorganization in the case of labor, the state can also encourage environmental and social disorganization. For example, the global south has suffered from what some have called the *resource curse*, an abundance of natural resources that instead of bringing prosperity to the region actually creates both ecological and social disorganization (Ross 1999). The extraction of resources can lead to armed conflicts. For example, Switzer (2002) demonstrates how much of the violent history of Sudan is related to the extraction of oil, while Shoko (2002) explains how small-scale mining and alluvial gold panning in the Zambezi river basin in Africa is likely to lead to future armed conflicts in the region.

An even more direct act by the state is to use existing ecological concerns to purposely create social disorganization. The elites in emerging economies can turn to natural resource scarcity (often the result of over-exportation) to further their stranglehold on their country. Kahl (1998: 87–8) provides an interesting example by arguing that state elites can use environmental distress to their advantage:

> To stay in power, all regimes, even the most authoritarian ones, require some base of social support. In a country experiencing severe democratic and environmental pressures, state elites are

likely to fear an erosion of this support if they are unable to meet the rising societal demands. Threats to a regime thus create incentives for state elites to search for strategies that will stabilize their base, mobilize new supporters, and co-opt or crush political opponents. Tragically, state elites often conclude that the instigation of intergroup violence is an effective means of achieving these goals.

So, not only does the extraction of natural resources often lead to violent conflicts, sometimes state elites take advantage of environmental stresses to retain power over their country. Homer-Dixon (1991: 77–8) provides a comprehensive list of ways that environmental change can lead to conflict, and these include: the global north and south fighting for wealth; conflict over the new Arctic trade route being created by climate change; population increases and related environmental stresses that can lead to "environmental refugees"; national conflicts over water and food supplies; and an overall increase in stress within national and international society that may lead to various types of unforeseen conflict. These examples suggest that existing ecological disorganization (that is often the result of the state's actions or inactions) will be purposely used to create social disorganization. The social disorganization is then used to destabilize the population, enabling the state to continue to rule with impunity. This process of state elites using environmental stress to solidify power can be considered a crime against the powerless because ordinary citizens are being manipulated into violent conflicts to help elites stay in power.

Downey, Bonds, and Clark (2010) suggest that natural resource extraction is often accompanied by armed violence. They point out that military conflict is not the only way to ensure natural resource extraction, suggesting instead that violence in general helps accomplish that goal. They suggest that the state facilitates this violence, and that global natural resource extraction is accomplished through the use of violence that is "controlled by military, policy, mercenary, and rebel forces from around the world that are usually, but not always, associated with local or national governments" (Downey *et al.* 2010: 418).

We argue that this may be extended to social disorganization; the forms of violence that accompany that disorganization may make the extraction of natural resources easy to carry out, and some corporations and states may exploit social disorganization to facilitate ecological disorganization and the accumulation of capital (Global Witness 2002).

Corporate actors

In demonstrating how closely the three pieces of the treadmill are intertwined, it is clear that in several ways, corporate actors encourage social disorganization involving both labor and the state. Corporations benefit, and have a hand in, many of the links between ecological and social disorganization that we have previously discussed. As noted earlier, corporations prefer to use the most efficient (cheapest) means of extraction and production, and one of the variable costs that they can reduce is labor. As chemical extraction and production technologies advance over time, so too does capital's insistence on their use; this leads to ecological disorganization and the subsequent loss of jobs and other forms of social disorganization.

The role of corporations in creating both ecological and social disorganization is arguably the greatest of the three actors in the treadmill. Since corporations are amoral, in that their only real goal is to maximize profits to satisfy shareholders, any environmental and social externalities that result from their action (or inaction), and that do not hinder the production process, do not get factored into the costs of production. Capital, therefore, will take advantage of anything that will increase profits. One of the great advantages that corporations hold is the mobility of capital and production. The ability to relocate production facilities, for example when labor becomes too expensive and state regulations on labor and the environment become too stringent, helps the treadmill continuing running at a rapid pace.

Decisions that are made by corporate actors to increase profits also increase environmental and social disorganization throughout the globe. The global relocation of production by corporate actors has led to what economists and political scientists have labeled "pollution havens," locations where pollution becomes concentrated due to a combination of factors that include lax environmental regulations and the availability of cheap labor (Cole 2004; Hall 2002; Strohm 2002). This process is one-directional, as pollution is moved from the global north to the global south, thereby increasing ecological disorganization in the south. In addition to the environmental problems that transnational relocation of pollution causes on the receiving countries, there are subsequent social disorganization problems that can arise as a result of the process.

One example of how ecological disorganization initiated by corporations leads to social disorganization is the case of population displacement caused by environmental stresses (Lonergan 1998; Opukri and Ibaba 2008). Forced migration, a crime against the powerless, is a complete disruption to a person's life and a community's existence. Recall that the traditional criminological definition of social disorganization theorizes that rapid transitions and immigration lead to an increase in street crime. The same argument can be used to explain this link between ecological and social disorganization. Migration due to environmental problems is widespread, leading one scholar to suggest that "environmental refugees have become the single largest class of displaced persons in the world" (Jacobson 1988); another estimates that by the year 2050 there will be approximately 150 million environmental refugees in the world (Myers 1993). This level of population displacement is sure to create large-scale social disorganization, as people are forced from their homes, villages, towns, and sometimes even countries. As people relocate in large numbers due to ecological disorganization such as deforestation, dumping of toxic waste, and violent conflict over scarce resources such as fresh water and arable land, social problems like unemployment, domestic violence, and other forms of conflict are likely to follow as the lives of families are thrown into total disarray (see also Agnew 2011).

Social disorganization and the treadmill

It is clear from the sections above that it is very difficult to isolate the effects of one of the treadmill actors without discussion of the others.

As previous chapters of this book have demonstrated, capitalism-based ecological disorganization is a complex and multifaceted process, in which labor, the state, and corporations all play significant roles. The same is true for social disorganization processes that are linked to (or are the direct result of) ecological disorganization.

In its initial conception, social disorganization theory was utilized to explain crime in communities, and that line of inquiry extends to social disorganization that is related to ecological disorganization, such as understanding the social impacts of natural resource extraction on local populations (Shoko 2002). Social disorganization that is related to ecological disorganization can also be observed beyond the community level, when examining the impacts on countries of large-scale violent conflict (Shoko 2002; Switzer 2002) and population displacement (Lonergan 1998; Opukri and Ibaba 2008). Understanding treadmill-induced social disorganization on the macro level is crucial because it is a structural approach to environmental problems, and social disorganization should be observed at the same level.

The treadmill of ecological and social disorganization

Schnaiberg (1980) created the concept of the ToP to explain how humans create environmental problems. In his early work the unit of analysis was the post-World War II United States. Subsequent work by Schnaiberg and his colleagues (Schnaiberg and Gould 1994; Gould et al. 2008) has extended the theory to explain how the treadmill now operates on a global level. This extension of treadmill theory was crucial for its development and continued relevance in the rapidly changing and globalized world. In this book, we hope to extend the reach of the treadmill framework by introducing it to a criminology audience and to demonstrate how this political economy perspective on green criminology is vital for unpacking why and how crimes against the environment are perpetrated. In addition, having focused on the relationship between ecological and social disorganization, this chapter intends to broaden the scope of treadmill research by demonstrating that not only does the treadmill process continue to damage ecosystems in ever greater amounts, but a major by-product of the treadmill is that it increases social harms as well.

We documented above examples of how ecological and social disorganization are related. This is an important addition to the treadmill literature because it demonstrates that the interplay between labor, the state, and corporate actors not only causes green crimes but also increases the level of social problems. Capitalism relies on continuous economic growth and expansion to produce beneficial results for labor, the state, and corporations, ignoring all negative environmental side effects. The same can be said about the relationship between capital and social problems that arise due to the operation of the treadmill; in the quest for economic growth, capitalism does not care if social ills result from the process of accumulation.

The three actors in the ToP *should* have reason to be concerned if capital accumulation processes cause social disorganization. While an extensive treatment of this topic is beyond the scope of this chapter, we now provide very brief examples of each.

In the case of labor, Marx (1867 [1976]) argued that the more the rate of surplus value expanded, the greater the exploitation of the labor. Capitalism produces social disorganization to enhance the rate of profit and the rate of surplus value extraction. It could be argued, then, that controlling/limiting social disorganization would benefit labor by reducing its exploitation. The state has obvious reasons for supporting the slowing of the treadmill to reduce the level of social disorganization. Social problems like unemployment (Cantor and Land 1985; Raphael and Winter-Ebmer 2001) often lead to street crimes, which can cause numerous problems for the state. Increases in street crime lead to the criminal justice system requiring more funding to combat crime, and an increase in the general disruption of societal functions, both of which the state has an interest in minimizing. Although slowing the treadmill is the opposite of the corporate goal of capital accumulation, corporate actors should be wary of social disorganization; large-scale social disorganization has the ability to slow the extraction and production processes if unemployment prevents the sale of products (Rifkin 1995). Or, for example, if an armed conflict erupts as the result of competition between corporate and local interests over natural resource extraction, this will slow the rate of resource extraction and therefore the rate of accumulation of profits, because the extraction process has been disrupted.

Based on these brief examples, it would seem that there are real possible threats to the three actors in the treadmill from social disorganization. However, the treadmill continues on unabated, as social disorganization is created in the search for economic growth. Both ecological and social disorganization, then, are seen (or more appropriately, not seen) by the treadmill actors as nothing more than unavoidable side effects of extraction, production, trade, retail, and consumption (i.e., the process of capitalism).

As theorized by Schnaiberg (1980), the treadmill is a continuous process because capitalism needs to have sustained economic growth in order for the system to continue working. Continuous economic growth requires continuous degradation of the natural environment, through natural resource extraction, land use conversions, etc. The economy grows, based partially on processes that cause ecological disorganization, and then the economy needs to grow more, necessitating more ecological disorganization, and so on. This process needs to constantly repeat for the treadmill to continue to run smoothly. Examining both ecological and social disorganization in the treadmill framework does not change the circular and repetitive path of the treadmill; rather, research has demonstrated that ecological disorganization causes social disorganization, and that social disorganization can then cause new ecological disorganization. Again, the process continually repeats itself.

Armed conflict can illustrate this process of ecological-social-ecological disorganization (or the treadmill of ecological and social disorganization). Earlier it was demonstrated that environmental issues/stresses can lead to social disorganization that results in armed conflict. We now look at the environmental consequences of armed conflict. Brauer (2011: 20) employs a typology created by Lanier-Graham (1993) to broadly classify the types of armed conflict related environmental damage:

1) intentional direct destruction of the environment during war;
2) incidental direct destruction, that is, collateral environmental

destruction incidental to war aims; and 3) induced destruction, that is, medium or long-term consequences directly attributable to war. The first category refers to the deliberate attack on cultivated and uncultivated lands and resources with the objective of environmental destruction for its own sake. The setting of oil-well fires by Iraq during the 1991 Persian Gulf War serves as an illustration. Examples of the second category include soil disturbance, as when troops dig trenches or when heavy equipment and battle tanks are ridden across fragile surfaces ... Damage in the third category, induced destruction, may occur as a result of human population shifts. Afghans fleeing to Iran and Pakistan, or Rwandans to eastern Congo, northern Burundi, and western Tanzania, can be expected to exert undue environmental stresses. Lack of sanitation and proper waste disposal can result in enormous amounts of untreated trash, and lack of shelter and fuel can result in deforestation.

These examples make it clear that war is extremely environmentally destructive, highlighting how social disorganization can create large-scale ecological disorganization (Foster *et al.* 2010). Schnaiberg's (1980) word "treadmill" is apt, both in his original ecological formulation of the ToP and in this new application, which shows how both ecological and social disorganization are the result of capitalism (and each other), and how environmental and social destruction continues unabated, along with the quest for unfettered economic growth.

Ecological and social disorganization and traditional crime

This chapter has focused on how the treadmill creates ecological and social disorganization. In the case of social disorganization, we have examined what we have called crimes against the working class, like increasing unemployment to expand the rate of surplus value, and crimes against the powerless, like forced migration. More traditional forms of crime, such as state-corporate crime and even street crime, can also be the result of the treadmill and ecological and social disorganization.

We now provide a few brief examples of how ecological and social disorganization can cause traditional crime.

Under capitalism, the state has the job of balancing the need for environmental protection and promoting economic growth. The state, particularly in the United States, primarily uses deterrence in the form of large financial penalties to discourage companies from violating environmental regulations on pollution like the Clear Air Act and the Clean Water Act. Stretesky, Long, and Lynch (2012) have argued that this process is ineffective, as large corporations are willing to pay the fines in order to keep polluting. The treadmill, then, runs on unhindered as corporations continue to collect capital, and create large amounts of ecological disorganization in the process. So even though companies who do not adhere to the environmental regulations are breaking the law, the financial penalties do not provide enough incentive to decrease production, and instead facilitate environmental additions like air and water pollution. It remains more profitable to continue to pollute, pay the fines to the government, so that production does not decrease.

In addition to not being effective in slowing ecological disorganization through the creation of criminal penalties, the state can create additional ecological disorganization when it directly engages in crime. State crime, which "consists of acts committed by state or government officials in the pursuit of their job as government officials" (Chambliss 1988: 327), can encourage practices that increase ecological disorganization. For example, Long *et al.* (2012) found that coal companies were more likely to donate to US federal political campaigns in the three-year period immediately prior to receiving an administrative, civil, or criminal sanction by the Environmental Protection Agency. It appears, therefore, that coal companies that are engaged in creating large amounts of ecological disorganization, as evidenced by the EPA violations, try to influence the outcome of their litigation by contributing money to politicians. The politicians who receive the campaign contributions and then act favorably toward the offending coal companies are committing state crimes that lead to increases in ecological disorganization. However, the crimes are not just those committed by actors of the state. As pointed out in Chapter 4, Kramer, Michalowski, and Kauzlarich (2002) expanded the concept of "state crime" to "state-corporate crime" in order to more fully capture the links between the state and corporate actors in their mutually beneficial criminal actions. So, the case of the coal company donations would be more accurately described as state-corporate crime. The corporate actors are primarily responsible for instigating the entire process because they are about to receive sanctions by the state, thereby slowing production (and the treadmill); this leads them to turn to campaign contributions to curry favor with agents of the state.

It is easy to see the links between ecological and social disorganization and state-corporate crime; however, the possible links to street crime should not be ignored. If we return to the example of mountaintop removal coal mining, the link between ecological and social disorganization and street crime becomes quickly apparent. After coal is extracted and a mine closes, former miners become unemployed. This social disorganization can lead to increases in violent crime like robbery, and property crime like burglary and larceny, as the former miners have lost their ability to support themselves and their families. This pattern of incidents is exactly what traditional social disorganization theory predicts in urban settings, but it is also happening in rural settings.

In addition, ecological disorganization is related to crime in ways that we have not previously imagined. Researchers are discovering that the production process may be creating pollution that impacts humans in a variety of ways, as suggested in Chapter 4. One important way that industrial pollution may be impacting humans is in the production of street crime. For example, exposure to contaminants such as lead may increase crime by disrupting neurotransmitters and altering behavior and thought patterns (Narag *et al.* 2009; Mielke and Zahran 2012; Needleman 2009; Stretesky and Lynch 2001). What criminologists suggest is that pollution is likely to change not only non-human elements of the ecosystem, but human elements as well, and this includes changes to behavior that make people more likely to engage in crime and violence. Researchers such as Stretesky and Lynch (2004) have also discovered that the relationship between lead and crime is not the same for all segments of the population; economically disadvantaged communities that lack resources are more likely to feel the crime-related effects of lead, suggesting that there is an environmental injustice in lead exposure and lead prevention efforts.

A research agenda for the treadmill of ecological and social disorganization

It is clear that there are widespread links between ecological and social disorganization in the areas of green crime, crimes against the working class, crimes against the powerless, state-corporate crime, violent crime, and property crime. However, this area of research remains neglected by criminologists and environmental sociologists. We believe that significant research can and should be conducted to unpack the links between ecological and social disorganization and crime.

Based on the discussions in this chapter, we propose that green criminologists should examine the following questions. First, when are increases in ecological disorganization related to increases in social disorganization? To date there have been very few studies of this relationship except as related to unequal exchange theory, and we encourage more work in the area. Second, do areas that suffer from both ecological and social disorganization have higher crime rates than areas that suffer from only one type of disorganization? We believe that this is likely to be the case, especially in rural crime where natural resource extraction may cause significant damage and destroy a community's social fabric.

We suggest that green criminologists can answer these questions by employing a variety of methods and levels of analysis, including neighborhood, community, city, state, country, and cross-national. Ecological disorganization, social disorganization, and crime data can be obtained for an equally diverse number of units of analysis, making for a broad research agenda in this area. The overlapping fields of green criminology, environmental sociology, and environmental science have a lot to contribute to this promising area of research.

6

THE TREADMILL
OF ANIMAL ABUSE

Animal abuse is one area of research in green criminology that has drawn considerable attention (e.g., Beirne 1999, 2007; Nurse 2013). Green criminology has opened academic space for criminologists interested in describing the extent of animal abuse, as well as the reasons for that abuse. Much of that research has drawn inspiration from a non-speciesist criminology that was formulated by Beirne (1999). Beirne's work focuses attention on non-human species as appropriate criminological subjects. Animal abuse research has also drawn on moral and philosophical approaches (Benton 1998).

While prior research has established some criteria for examining animal abuse within the general framework of green criminology, it has been noted that there is some theoretical tension in these approaches. A significant portion of the green criminological literature examines animal abuse (e.g., Nurse 2013), much of which examines animal abuse without sufficient rationale or criteria for including animals as appropriate subject matter for green criminology. Because green criminology does not generally address the rationale for the specific inclusion of animal abuse as appropriate subject matter, the study of animal abuse appears to occupy a privileged position within this emerging discipline. That privileged position makes it appear that the study of animal abuse and green criminology are practically synonymous. What has not been addressed in green criminological discussions of animal harms is whether animals ought to occupy such a privileged space in green criminology. Given the definitions of green criminology and green crime that have emerged within criminology – and we realize that there are several competing definitions – the question is whether the examination of animal abuse and harms fits within those definitions. This question has been previously recognized by Beirne (2007), who offers reasons for both the inclusion and exclusion of animal harm research within green criminology.

As Beirne (2007) points out, the study of animal abuse and harm presents a theoretical problem for green criminology that has not been adequately addressed. That problem involves aligning a definition of green crime with the study of animal abuse. Recall that we defined green crimes in Chapter 1 as those acts that cause significant harm to ecosystems to support and maintain production. This creates a problem for green criminologists who wish to study animal abuse because animals may be abused in a variety of ways and for a variety of reasons that may not be related to ecological harm. There is a clear difference between the harms animals suffer when, for example, a wetland is destroyed or a wooded area is deforested, or a mountaintop is removed for the purposes of mining, compared to the abuse of animals on corporate farms. Thus, the latter forms of animal abuse do not appear to involve the kinds of harm to ecosystems that are compatible within green criminology. Beirne (2007) recognizes these definitional problems and suggests that the forms of animal abuse that fit within green criminology have not been defined sufficiently. In making that argument, Beirne points out that green criminology has yet to establish definitional parameters or theoretical concerns that distinguish its inclusion of animal abuse or its approach to animal abuse from research in related fields. As Beirne notes, there is currently significant overlap between the kinds of animal abuse research undertaken within green criminology, animal studies, and human-animal studies. Nevertheless, it is unclear why the study of animal abuse ought to be included within green criminology, or why such studies are not more properly situated within the animal studies or human-animal studies literatures.

From a green criminological perspective, one way to address this problem is simply to note that *some* kinds of animal harm and abuse studies are relevant to green criminology because they are related to ecosystems. However, such a definition would exclude a wide range of animal abuse and harm studies as green crime related and exclude them from the green criminological literature. This is, to be sure, a simple way to address the issue of what kinds of animal studies belong within the green criminological literature.

Given the focus of this book on the ToP, we argue that animal harm is related to the political economy because there is a relationship between animals and the economy. The purpose of this chapter, then, is to make a specific link between animal abuse and political economic theories that can be extended to the study of the ecology and the environment. This is the same argument we made in Chapter 5 when examining human suffering and reviewing how ecological disorganization and processes that cause ecological disorganization can lead to social disorganization. In short, the ToP provides one way to examine animal harms and abuse as pertinent and related to the framework of green criminology. Importantly, treadmill theory allows for an explanation of animal abuse that is situated in a political economic perspective. This chapter is designed to explore that connection by examining how the political economy is related to animal abuse specifically by drawing upon notions of energy presented in Chapter 2. More specifically, we describe how the treadmill is related to animal abuse by examining how the treadmill produces various outcomes through the conversion of natural spaces into human habitats, the extraction of raw materials, the processing of waste streams, toxic waste disposal, and the use of animals as commodities. We draw upon two case studies to demonstrate these concepts in action.

The production of animal abuse

Green criminologists take up the study of animal harms for different reasons. Thus, there is no unifying theoretical orientation in the animal abuse literature produced by green criminologists, and this often leaves the reader feeling confused about why animal abuse is examined within green criminology. In short, green criminologists have not offered a convincing or uniform theoretical rationale for including animal abuse research within green criminology. In this sense, we see our preference for a political economic explanation of animal abuse as overcoming the existing limitations of the extant literature on animal abuse in green criminology. Our goal is to illustrate how animal abuse research is consistent with green criminology and the political economy of environmental harm, crime, law, and justice. We contend that for animal abuse studies to comprise one of the aspects of green criminological research, the fit between animal abuse studies and the scope of green criminology must be clarified. As a result, we see production as central in that effort.

Political economy

Humans commit a vast array of harms against animals. It is our contention that not all of those animal harms are appropriate subject matter for green criminology, as many are unrelated to green crime. For example, people who harm animals may exhibit some form of psychological disturbance, or display patterns of antisocial and violent behaviors (Arluke *et al.* 1999; Flynn 1999). These are not the forms of animal abuse that ought to concern green criminologists. In our view, in order to be included within green criminology, studies of animal abuse must demonstrate how the ToP produces animal harms. This demonstration, then, must include references to the political economy. Green criminologists should seek to discover the political economic structures within a society that lead to the widespread and persistent abuse of animals, and the forces behind the regularity of those forms of abuse.

Consider the issue of animal experimentation that often involves harm and death to experimental animals. Individual-level explanations for such abuse may depict scientists as engaging in animal abuse because of some personality defect. Yet, there is little reason to believe that scientists harm animals because all scientists who work with animals share some group psychological defect. Indeed, from prior research we know that scientists will often engage in animal research with reluctance (Herzog 1993). Whatever their degree of reluctance, scientists view animal experiments as the only way to produce the kinds of knowledge that would improve health and safety (Botting and Morrison 1993). In contrast to the idea that the abuse of experimental animals is a result of defective psychological states – though that is certainly the case sometimes – we see the structure and political economy of science and its practice as generating a routine form of animal abuse that characterizes animal experimentation. Focusing attention on the individual abusers, then, misses the real issue – the structural context that leads to the abuse of experimental animals. Scientists are bound by rules that specify given procedures. These procedures, which decide how animals will be treated, are not determined by individual scientists, but by the guidelines that have become regular practice. What is important and interesting is how animal abuse is subsumed within the structural dimensions of social, economic, and political relations.

In our view, the political economy is one of the forces structuring scientific requirements. That is to say, it is not the merits of science, nor the scientific method itself, that serve as an objective yardstick that determines how science is practiced. Instead, science is employed for such things as the creation of testing protocols or to measure health and safety and to establish regulatory safety limits, and the guidance offered by science may come into conflict with the interests of producers. Ideally, in such matters, the guidance offered by science should receive preference. For example, if science tells us that the health exposure threshold for a chemical is x units (e.g., 10 micrograms per deciliter), then that is the standard that law should allow. But, as explained in Chapter 3, the law does not work this way because law is anything but an objective measure of harm (Hillyard et al. 2004). Rather than being an objective measure of harm, law is a social construction that registers the amount and kinds of harm that the social forces that make law are willing to allow. In the case of environmental law, politicians that create the law strike an "agreement" between the science of harm and the interests of producers, in moving the measure of harm as far away as possible from the scientific measure of harm. This environmental law-making process is not, in reality, an agreement with which all sides are pleased. The regulations that result from that process can only be seen as an agreement to the extent that the legal result lies somewhere in between the parameters of harm defined by the different parties involved, in the effort to set a health standard for environmental pollution or for the kinds and numbers of animals that can be used in an experiment.

Following the logic above, the political economic process that impacts the making of rules related to scientific experimentation makes animal experiments acceptable forms of animal abuse. There is, for instance, a broad array of political economic interests in facilitating and maintaining animal experimentation (Groves 1994). The laboratory animal business in the US generates hundreds of millions of dollars annually within biotechnology, pharmaceuticals, biomedical, commercial, and government industries (Groves 1996). It is, therefore, not the manifestation of the experimental animal harms that ought to draw our attention, but rather the structural network of relationships that produced the need for those harms to exist in the first place – that is, the political economic treadmill of animal abuse.

A political economic approach to animal abuse provides one way of including some forms of animal abuse within green criminology. In framing our view on this point, we are drawing upon the discussions in Chapter 2, which examined the ToP and the political economy of ecological disorganization, and more specifically environmental destruction. As a reminder of that position we note that O'Connor (1998: 5) observes that in today's global capitalist economy, the forces of capital have organized the world so that the "capitalist cycle and the exploitation of labor are privileged over the life cycle of organisms." This remark is useful to the extent that it begins to establish a framework for equating the exploitation of animals within a larger political economic theory of capitalism.

Animal abuse: from the psychological to the structural

One way in which to situate animal abuse within the political economy of green harms and to reflect the assumptions of political economic theory reviewed in Chapter 2 is to examine the physics of work. In doing so it is possible to develop an explanation of the relationship between animal abuse and the political economy of green crime.

Throughout history, humans have used animals to intensify and replace human labor, and to make the labor process more efficient. This tendency to employ animals for this purpose, while not an invention of capitalism, expanded along with the advance of capitalism and its efforts to reduce the use of human labor in the process of production. Under capitalism, the use of animal labor took on new dimensions as part of the machinery of labor (Hribal 2003).

It is likely, as Beirne (2007) notes, that humans have abused animals in various ways throughout history. That history of abuse, though not taken up or elucidated in the animal abuse literature, proceeds as if the modern manifestation of animal abuse is a product of psychological aberration, and this has always been the driving force behind animal abuse throughout the ages. For example, in criminology and psychological studies, animal abuse has been treated as an individual-level manifestation of psychological and personality deficits (Agnew 1998), and in that view, animal abuse is interpreted as a pathway to forms of abuse "that matter" – the transition of an animal abuse history into human-directed aggression (Arluke *et al.* 1999). Such a view fails to appreciate the independent significance of animal abuse detached from animal abuse's interpretation as a gateway phenomenon (i.e., as a pathway to human abuse), and overlooks the structural dimensions of animal abuse in favor of reductionist forms of psychological explanations, a view well criticized by Mills (1959).

If this psychological view is correct, then given the persistence and widespread nature of animal abuse, its routine appearance ought to be able to explain a significant amount of human aggression, and this view would have broad cross-cultural support and rank highly among those factors that cause crime. As a result, animal abuse and the distribution and quantity of human violence ought to be very highly correlated. To be sure, there is some evidence that human violence and animal abuse are correlated (Nurse 2013). However, animal abuse is one among many explanations for violence. Therefore, in contrast to that psychological view of animal abuse as gateway behavior it is necessary to understand animal abuse as an independent phenomenon, and given its widespread manifestations, as a structural rather than an individual-level outcome. One way of getting at the structural roots of animal abuse is to investigate animal abuse in its association to larger structural forces and dynamics.

General forms of animal abuse and political economy

In taking a political economic view of the use of animals in production by humans, we posit that routinized animal abuse stems from animals' relationship to energy and work. The physics of the work process and its connection to capitalist systems of production can be employed to establish the basis for a political economic interpretation of animal abuse. One form of animal abuse is related to production and the extraction of animal labor power. Another form of animal abuse occurs when they threaten production and therefore must be exterminated. For example, as "beasts of burden," animal labor is used to contribute to production, while in some cases animals also become commodities or are transformed into commodities by human economic relations. We explore each of these issues in more detail.

Animal labor power and abuse

As workers and commodities, animals can be abused in a number of ways. Beirne (2007), for example, provides a historical example of animals abused by workers and servants. This kind of animal abuse is not simply a manifestation of some psychological state, but rather is a reflection of the interconnection of humans and animals in the political economy of production. In a political economic sense, animals are used to provide labor or as commodities. As commodities, the animal is a direct vessel for value, and when workers focus their physical aggression on animals, they do so to strike out in direct ways against those who control the labor process and who own animals.

Animals can also contribute labor to the political economic system of production and, in this role, animal labor power can be employed to intensify and replace human labor. By intensifying and replacing human labor, animal labor becomes part of the machinery of capitalism. In this context we must keep in mind that those who controlled the labor process introduced animals into that process to reduce costs and intensify labor. As a result, animals can represent a threat to labor in various ways. The use of animal labor, for example, reduces the need for human labor, and thus marginalizes labor, and in this regard has the ability to produce a surplus of human labor (Marx 1976 [1867]). That surplus of human labor combined with the use of animal labor can act to reduce the value of human labor to its minimum requirement. This process helps maintains human labor at subsistence levels, and forces the laboring class to live out a life in impoverished conditions. In this productive context, then, one can understand the abuse of animals as an outcome of productive relationships. The abuse of animals may be interpreted as a form of worker rebellion against their masters or others who employ their labor, and animal abuse serves as one way in which those relations become manifest, a possibility previously identified by Beirne (2007).

The importance of animal labor in production and as a source of physical power employed to operate that system can be seen in efforts to measure work in output terms defined by animal labor capabilities. Historically, by the time mechanical advances were being introduced to intensify labor and reduce production costs, animals such as horses had became very valuable components of the labor process. Illustrating that point, James Watt, inventor of the steam engine in the eighteenth century, spent considerable effort calculating the *horsepower* equivalent output of the steam engine he had invented in order to demonstrate its work-saving attributes (Hart 2006). The measure of horsepower Watt created continues to be used in the contemporary world to describe the volume of work and amount of power machinery can produce.

Modern science estimates, for instance, that one horsepower produces about 745.7 watts of energy (Hart 2006). Employing other known scientific standards, that volume of energy can be translated into other measures of power equivalents. Using that information, it is possible to estimate that the energy equivalent to one horsepower is equal to the amount of sustainable work that ten people can perform. In other words, one horse could perform sufficient labor to replace ten human laborers, while a one horsepower steam engine could replace the labor of one horse or ten humans.

As technological innovations improved the efficiency of the steam engine and led to the development of other forms of engines such as the combustion engine, machinery that burned fossil fuels could increasingly be employed to replace human and animal labor, acting to both intensify labor and reduce the costs of production. The extent to which fossil fuel use can replace labor can be illustrated employing scientific calculations of the power produced by burning fossil fuels. For example, burning one gallon of diesel fuel produces the equivalent of 54.33 horsepower, or 54.33 horses. And thus one gallon of fossil fuel can be used to replace the labor of roughly 543.3 humans.

We believe that there are a number of forms of animal abuse that occur because of their economic benefits and losses, and these are a structural outcome of economic relations. These forms of animal cruelty and abuse, because of their association with economic forces that penetrate society, are likely the predominant forms of animal abuse that occur within a society, and will relate to the abuse of animals in productive roles (e.g., treating animals as commodities and abusing them to increase their production and reproduction and minimize the cost of raising commodity animals; the treatment of animals, such as laboratory animals, that provide labor by serving as scientific commodities, etc.). This hypothesis about animal abuse would be empirically testable if governments or other groups maintained sufficient records on the variety of ways in which animals are abused.

The destruction of animals that limit accumulation

Animals are not only objects of abuse when they can be used to facilitate capital accumulation or transfer value from nature to humans through work. Animals can also be abused in various ways when they act as impediments to capital accumulation. In contrast to accumulative animal abuse, some animals may be hunted and abused because they hinder economic activity; as impediments to economic growth, these animals are abused to protect economic investments (Fogleman 1989). In their roles as "predators" and "grazers", or as actors that destroy capital, animals are operating according to their nature, but are defined as drains on the potential of individuals to realize the surplus value of their productive practices when animals essentially act as non-paying consumers or thieves. Creating hunting regulations related to the taking of economically destructive species, or variances from hunting rules to allow farmers to execute economically destructive wild animals (sometimes even when they are endangered), serve as relevant examples. Consider the following:

> Efficacy of Compound 1080 LP Collars was studied under pen and field conditions. Coyotes poisoned themselves by attacking collared sheep and biting the collars. In 54 pen tests where 1 or 2 captive coyotes had opportunity to attack 1 collared lamb, 41 lambs were attacked and 26 collars were punctured. Of 25 different coyotes offered lambs with collars containing 5 or 10 mg sodium fluoroacetate (FAC)/ml, 23 coyotes attacked and 21 died after collars were punctured in their first (n = 17), second (n = 3), or fifth (n = 1) test. For 11 captive coyotes that punctured rubber collars, the average time to death was 217 min (range 115 to 436 min [cited in Connolly and Burns 1990: 1]).

As this passage demonstrates, wild animals such as coyotes can limit capital accumulation when they become "pests" that prey upon livestock, destroy agriculture, or become nuisance animals that interfere with the human population's routine activities that contribute to the social and economic order of capitalism's economic arrangements.

From a political economic perspective, these two general forms of animal abuse are important because of their connection to the ToP and consumption, an issue explored in the sections that follow. In our view, the ToP also establishes a treadmill of animal abuse, or the persistent abuse of animals as a structural outcome of the operation of the ToP.

Types of animal abuse from an ecological perspective

In our interpretation of the political economy or treadmill of animal abuse, the routine nature of animal abuse is connected to the role of animals in political economy, which will impact the volume of animal abuse, as well as the types of animal abuse that emerge historically or across cultures. From these general observations, we can now examine various forms of contemporary animal abuse in relation to political economy and provide a number of examples that support this hypothesized relationship.

It is not difficult to illustrate that a variety of contemporary forms of animal abuse fit within green criminology when the political economic focus of green criminology is applied to explaining factors that promote animal abuse. For example, the use and expansion of animal laboratory testing, the vast animal experimentation production complex that now exists, and the use of experimental animals to develop and test pharmaceutical and other medical advances provide clear examples of how political economy affects the promotion of green crimes of violence against laboratory animals.

To this list of green crimes of animal abuse one can add an array of offenses influenced by political economic factors (Nurse 2013). These offenses include harms to animals produced by habitat destruction that occurs when humans convert lands from their natural uses to human uses; by over-fishing of wild populations of fish treated as universal food stocks supplied by nature; by the genetic modification of animals and livestock to enhance their production and food reproduction value in ways that make these animals "better" commodities (Walters 2007); by the cruel conditions in animal food-processing plants and on factory farms employed to increase production of food; by the illegal animal trade and the trade in animal parts used to create markets for such commodities to facilitate accumulation; by the use and mistreatment of animals related to circuses, in animal acts, zoos, in the entertainment industry, and in the production of leisure services such as carriage rides, which are used to transfer accumulated capital (Nurse 2013).

This section describes the routine specific types of contemporary animal abuse that can be linked to political economic forces. As noted in Chapter 2, the treadmill not only pushes production, it also continuously increases the rate of natural resource extraction and the addition of pollution to ecosystems. The ToP has a significant impact on the environment. Within production, resource extraction and pollution cause significant environmental damage that impact species inhabiting natural ecosystems. Countless animal species (as well as other non-animal species and humans) are impacted by these treadmill outcomes. Thus, these various species become victims of the treadmill. Animal harms related to the ToP are the result of five processes:

1   the conversion of natural spaces into human habitats;
2   the extraction of raw materials;
3   toxic waste spills;
4   toxic waste disposal; and
5   the inclusion of animal species as commodities.

The kinds of animal harms associated with each of these five processes are briefly described below.

Conversion of natural space

Treadmill harms include the conversion of natural space to human use, which comes in a variety of forms. Of the natural spaces that may be converted to human spaces, some are much more environmentally sensitive and important as natural spaces than others. Regardless of their importance in maintaining ecological equilibrium and the conditions for life for various species, all natural spaces play some role in maintaining the health of the overall world ecological system. The natural spaces humans convert to human use include but are not limited to the following: waterfronts (oceans, bays, rivers, streams, lakes and ponds), wetland areas, prairie, mountains and hills, forests and barren areas, ecological transition areas (dunes, scrubs), tundra, and desert. In terms of green criminology, political economy and animal abuse, the primary concern is the relationship between treadmill land conversion and habitat loss as a form of animal abuse. The process of treadmill land conversion may transform the ability of a natural area to support natural species, leading to declining populations or the extinction of species. Treadmill land conversion may also lead to the killing of local species, producing direct forms of animal abuse that stem from political economic relations. These direct forms of abuse may occur when species are killed when areas are bulldozed; or perish when explosives or burning are employed to clear the land for development; when various species are crushed by heavy equipment and construction-related vehicles used to clear and prepare land for development; when immature members of a species are separated from their parents by the process of development; or killings that may result when species are removed from waterways by dredging; or when they are suffocated by the backfilling of wetland areas. This type of abuse is widespread and often directly destroys ecosystems and their components and can be thought of as a green crime.

The extraction of raw materials

As noted in Chapter 3, the physical process of extracting raw materials from ecosystems may produce extensive disruption to the environment and may result in animal abuse. Some of these effects are similar to those incurred by the conversion of natural space into human spaces. As an example, the practice of mountaintop removal in mining, with its use of extraordinarily large heavy machinery and its reliance on explosives, is likely to kill and maim local wildlife, and destroy their habitat and food sources (Wilcove and Wikelski 2008). Many common resource extraction techniques reconfigure the environment and make it less hospitable for local wildlife. For example, above-ground structures used in some resource extraction practices create barriers to the movement of local wildlife, preventing them from accessing their normal range or engaging in routine animal activities including migration. In addition, many resource extraction practices involve the use of chemicals to extract resources, and produce extensive and quite harmful waste streams that pollute and even poison local environments and the species that inhabit those environments. In this way, the political economy of raw material extraction generates treadmill-processing waste streams, which become a unique form of treadmill animal abuse.

Toxic waste spills

The extraction and processing of raw materials creates an extensive toxic waste stream, as discussed in Chapter 4. These waste streams exist in different forms and in various locations in the extraction of raw material, and create a geographic network of toxins and waste. As an example, the mining and on-site processing of coal generates liquid toxic waste-processing streams (Tiwary 2001). Those wastes are impounded near coal extraction sites in large liquid waste lagoons. It has been estimated that more than 1,300 such sites exist across the natural landscape of the US. Those treadmill waste sites contain large quantities of harmful toxic waste. In the US it is estimated that coal processing produces 7,300 tons (14.6 million pounds) of heavy metal wastes (i.e., mercury, nickel, beryllium, cadmium, arsenic, and selenium) that are contained in above-ground impoundments (Keating et al. 2000). Those heavy metal wastes pose significant threats to local water sources. And when such lagoon impoundments overflow or break, significant environmental damage is created.

Coal ash impoundments contain not only dangerous metal waste but the processing chemicals used to clean coal, and, of course, coal ash suspended in the waste waters used for processing. If the metal wastes are estimated to be in excess of 14 million pounds, the volume of all waste found in coal ash lagoons is several times larger, and likely contains hundreds of millions of pounds of coal ash and other waste products. As evidence of the problem these coal ash lagoons present, consider that there have been a number of significant coal ash spills from lagoon impoundments and coal ash pipelines in the US in recent years. These include those that have occurred in the following locations:

- Luke, Maryland; March, 2009; 4,000 gallons; contents of the spill contained coal ash from a waste pipeline. The affected area includes the Chesapeake River.
- Harriman, Tennessee; December, 2008; 1.7 million yards (1.1 billion gallons) of coal ash waste from an impoundment. The spill affected 400 acres that included Swan Pond, Watts Bar Lake, and Emory River. The spill covered homes and also caused a train derailment. In terms of volume, this spill was 180 times larger than the oil spill caused by the Exxon Valdez disaster in Prince William Sound.
- Stevenson, Alabama; January, 2009; 10,000 gallons of coal ash. The spill affected an area that included Widows Creek and the Tennessee River.
- Martin County, Kentucky; October, 2000; 250 million gallons of coal sludge. The affected area included Cold Water Creek and Wolf Creek as well as the Big Sandy River. This spill was 30 times larger than the *Exxon Valdez* oil spill.
- Oak Creek Power Plant, Wisconsin; October, 2011; 2,500 cubic yards or 202,500 yards of waste 1 foot deep of coal ash. The affected area included Lake Michigan. This spill was about 20 times larger than the *Exxon Valdez* oil spill.

It should be kept in mind that waste spills of the magnitude described above cannot be easily or efficiently remediated, and evidence of those spills are likely to remain in the environment for hundreds of years. For example, more than 20 years after the *Exxon Valdez* oil spill, significant deposits of liquid and tar oils can be found below the surface of beaches, and these appear to be harming otters as they search for food (Bodkin *et al.* 2012).

Generally, environmental agencies are concerned with the human effects such spills might produce, and little attention is paid to the effects of these spills on wildlife species – at least by government agencies. These spills, however, will tend to have the same kinds of effects for non-human species, and those effects are likely to be magnified in wild species, given their proximity to the waste and the decreased physical size of those species relative to humans. The kinds of massive waste spills described here destroy wild species' habitats, and the ecological system those species depend upon. Moreover, animals may be buried alive in the rush of coal ash spills, and if they survive the spill may find that they cannot successfully return to their home territories, now covered in coal ash and polluted beyond use. In addition, these spills leave behind a toxic legacy that will affect the health of wild species for several generations.

Toxic waste disposal

The ToP creates a very large volume of toxic waste that requires disposal. As noted above, some of that waste is produced on site at resource extraction facilities, contaminating local areas and presenting the same kinds of health consequences for animals as it does for humans, if not more intense. Such noxious waste pollution may produce large fish kills in lakes, streams, and rivers, and so badly pollute local waterways that they affect the food chain. These wastes are not limited to liquid wastes, and mining operations often produce significant quantities of toxic solid waste detrimental to animal populations. In addition, significant volumes of toxic waste are generated by the production processes where raw materials are converted into products. These toxins also pose significant health threats to wild animal populations.

Pollution has a broad geographic scope. Natural resources extracted through treadmill resource extraction processes are shipped to manufacturers, and processed into commodities. That production process generates more waste, which is emitted into the environment. Such emissions come in different forms, and may include solid wastes, air pollution, water pollution, and wastes that are injected underground. These waste products are not immobile, and once emitted may travel significant distances, impacting the environment far from the urban centers where such wastes are produced. Indeed, scientific evidence suggests that industrial wastes associated with the treadmill process of production show up in locations quite distant from human population centers. Sea species living far from human populations show evidence of these pollutants (Sindermann 1979), as do land species in isolated locations such as Siberia (Kim *et al.* 1996), and the North Pole (Corsolini *et al.* 2006). In this way, the treadmill creates widespread forms of animal abuse linked to the ToP.

Animals as commodities

Animals are abused not only as a consequence of how things are made and how toxic waste is disposed, but also via their role as commodities. Animals are harmed by the treadmill when they are harvested from nature as specimens for scientific purposes or for display and experimentation, or as food, as pets, as zoo animals, or for parts of animals that humans may use as "medicine," or for other purposes. In addition, the treadmill facilitates the production of significant animal populations raised for food (Mallon 2005; Mosel 2001). These animals, because they are raised for food and because the purpose of such activity is profit oriented, are often housed in deplorable conditions that constitute abuse. Moreover, in the process of turning those animals into food products, they may not only be treated inhumanely, but also killed in inhumane ways (Warrick 2001). Laboratory animals may be placed in inhumane conditions either in the process of being raised, or in the experimental conditions in which they are employed.

It should be evident from the above that a significant volume of animal abuse in the modern world has political economic origins. The fact that a broad range of forms of animal abuse can be linked to political economic explanation and forces is in itself a sufficient reason to examine the political economy of animal abuse. Moreover, as was argued above, the political economy of animal abuse provides one mechanism for distinguishing the kinds of animal abuse issues that green criminology includes, and for differentiating those studies from those in related areas of animal abuse research.

Treadmill of animal abuse case studies

The political economy of animal abuse, or the treadmill of animal abuse and harm, is, as illustrated above, widespread. We have provided a general description of those harms, and in the sections that follow we illustrate, through case studies, some of the specific ways in which animals are harmed by the ToP.

Tortoises and turtles

One general example of the effect of the treadmill on animal abuse is the trade in exotic animals and animal parts. A number of studies have examined these issues (Alaca and George 2008; Du Bois 1997; Warchol *et al.* 2003), including the poaching of wild animal species (Lemieux and Clarke 2009; Pires and Clarke 2012, 2011). There are many other instances of these animal harms, some of which may be less well known or publicized, and these include the effect of the ToP on turtles.

Professor of biology Craig B. Stanford (2010) estimates that every year 10 million turtles and tortoises are traded in Asian nations. In China alone the turtle trade is estimated to be a $700 million dollar industry. The problem, Stanford notes, is that the majority of those turtles and tortoises come from the wild, and the practice of harvesting wild turtles and tortoises from their habitats has a dramatic impact on the environment as well as on the kidnapped species and the individuals from those species.

The trade in turtles and tortoises is not limited to Asian nations. Many individual animals in these species end up in the US and Europe as part of the pet trade market or as a specialized part of the treadmill. The trade in turtles and tortoises is extensive, and as Stanford notes, "The point is, turtles and tortoises have become a global trade item" (2010: 3). In political economic terms, turtles and tortoises are part of the global system of capitalism, and are severely impacted by the portion of the treadmill related to marketing wild animals for various uses.

In the process of becoming global commodities, turtles and tortoises face numerous serious forms of animal abuse: "We cut down their forests, hunt them for food and profit, take them from their mothers and lock them in shocking conditions of confinement, and generally regard them as food, toys and threats ... they are ... expendable commodities, nothing more than pieces of meat or currency exchange" (Stanford 2010: 6). As Stanford notes, turtles and tortoises have long been used in this way, and the best available evidence of humans using turtles for food and other purposes traces this practice back 8,600 years (2010: 12). Yet, despite this long history, turtles and tortoises were never as much in danger as they are in the modern capitalist world system, with its unyielding ToP and consumption that has expanded the market for these species.

In the modern ToP, turtles and tortoises lose out in many ways. Significant losses, for example, accrue because of real estate development. In the US, for example, those who develop real estate simply have to pay a one-time fine to bulldoze and destroy turtle habitat (Stanford 2010: 62–84). Turtles and tortoises lose habitat to deforestation and wetland destruction, and in areas already under development, to roadways, which not only destroy their habitat but also expose them to becoming road-kill victims.

In the modern world economy, turtles and tortoises are part of the system of trade. But as a natural species, in some locations they also stand in the way of development. If, for instance, a turtle species becomes so rare that it is defined as endangered, it can halt human efforts to develop nature in its tracks. In cases where these species have become identified as endangered, this identification can promote their abuse and illegal harvest, a condition that can be tied to the larger ToP and the emphasis capitalism generates by associating supply rarity and price.

Worldwide, the trade in turtles and tortoises as food, as pets, and for their parts is a multi-billion-dollar part of the ToP. This international ToP related to turtles and tortoises is part of the capitalist world system. As part of that treadmill, people in poor and underdeveloped nations, exploited by capital for their labor and resources, do not receive fair value for their labor, and are not empowered by increased access to the means of production. These international inequities, supported by the world treadmill process, help to maintain poor and underdeveloped nations as poor and underdeveloped. At the same time, the international capitalist system imports values conducive to expectation of success into those locations. Increasingly deprived of access to their traditional lifestyles by the destruction of local natural resources by the international treadmill and, at the same time expecting to advance economically and dealing with the problems of subsistence living the treadmill imposes by destroying and exporting local natural resources, people in poor and underdeveloped nations must create new ways to survive. Some of those new behaviors add to the threats faced by species such as turtles and tortoises, which are used to satisfy local demand for food, to provide jobs, hunting and collecting turtles for export, in nations where jobs are scarce and the international ToP has excluded those populations from any meaningful way of life.

Corporate animal farming

Another prime contemporary example of the intersection of capital's ToP and animal abuse is found in the corporate animal farm. Livestock production is no longer the domain of family farms; rather, enormous corporate factory farms dominate meat production in the United States. Estimates suggest that less than a century ago, approximately 80 per cent of the US population was involved in agriculture; that figure is now around 2 per cent (Havercamp 1998). Furthermore, an estimated 300,000 family farms disappeared between 1979 and 1998 (HFA 2012). These decreases in the number of individuals employed in agriculture and the number of family farms comes at a time when population is increasing, so it is not that there are fewer customers; rather, the nature of the meat industry has changed, moving from small family farms to large corporate factory farms (also known as Concentrated Animal Feeding Operations).

The increase and eventual domination of the US meat industry by factory farms has brought with it a marked increase in the abuse of animals that are raised for human consumption. Factory farms view animals as commodities that are to be sold for profit, and the fact that they are living creatures is of no concern to the operators of the farms. This commodity perspective of the farmers translates into horrible abuses and living conditions forced upon the animals in order to reduce production costs and increase yields (Mallon 2005; Mosel 2001).

All animals that are factory farmed are subject to myriad abuses; however, for illustration purposes we focus on cows and chickens.

Warrick (2001) details the story of Ramon Moreno, an employee at a Washington State meat-packing plant. It was Ramon's job to cut off the legs of cows as they were moved along the assembly line. The cows were supposed to be unconscious by the time they made it to Ramon's station, but often that was not the case, and Ramon was forced to remove the limbs of live cows (Mallon 2005). Factory farm owners are driven by production and anything that slows down production, such as checking that the cows are dead before their legs are cut off, is viewed as unacceptable. Cows in factory farms are also fed large doses of antibiotics to cause them to increase their weight, and they are forced to eat "remains of sick cattle, chicken manure, human sewage, rendered meat, ground bone meal and 40 billion pounds worth of slaughterhouse waters like blood, bone, and viscera, as well as the remains of millions of euthanized cats and dogs" (Machado 2003: 809), instead of their traditional diet of grass (Mallon 2005: 20). This forced diet serves to help reduce waste that comes from other parts of the farm.

The case of chickens is no better. After chickens are hatched in a factory farm, the females (who are used for egg production) are separated from the males. Since the males have no value, they are discarded and put into large plastic bags; they consequently "suffocate under the weight of other chicks dumped on top on them" (Fox 1995: 151). Furthermore, chickens live in cages that are not big enough for them to turn around and they "may spend their entire lives without even fully stretching their wings" (Mosel 2001: 6). The farmers manipulate the light in the chicken coops to encourage egg production around the clock. The stressful conditions that the chickens are forced to live under often produce cannibalistic behavior (Mosel 2001).

It is clear that cows, chickens, and other factory farm-raised animals (such as pigs and veal calves) are abused by factory farmers. When animals are transformed from living creatures into commodities, produced and sold for profit by the ToP, abuse follows. This type of abuse affects a much larger number of animals than those who are abused by people with psychological problems, which leads us to argue that animal abuse on corporate factory farms is the most widespread form of animal abuse in the world.

Summary

We began this chapter by questioning the extent to which animal harms and abuse belong in the study of green criminology. One of the leading experts on animal abuse studies in criminology, Piers Beirne, has noted that there has been a failure to better integrate green criminological research on animal harms with studies of animal harms from other disciplines. We noted that definitions of green criminology appear to preclude the study of experimental animal harms as fitting green criminology's focus on environmental harms. We then amended this position, arguing that experimental or other kinds of animal abuse studies fit within the parameters of green criminology when animal abuse and harms can be explained with reference to production and political economic theory.

Consistent with our understanding of green criminology as promoting political economic studies of environmental harms, and the focus of this book on the ToP, this chapter has laid out one way of facilitating the inclusion of the study of animal abuse and harms within green criminology. To be sure, there are forms of animal abuse and harm that our approach excludes at this point, such as the psychological aspect of animal abuse, or individual-level manifestations of animal abuse. Until such a time that researchers can offer a sufficient political economic approach to those problems, we suggest that those kinds of studies are best omitted from the purview of green criminology and the definition of green crime. Instead, we propose that green criminologists focus on animal abuse related to production.

This chapter has illustrated how the treadmill of production creates significant forms and volumes of animal abuse that can be examined as connected to green crimes. There is certainly much work that remains to be done employing the view we have set forth in this chapter. Thus, far from being a dead issue, we see much hope for the development of a unique green criminological approach to the study of animal abuse and harm that is connected to political economic theory and explanations such as the ToP and consumption.

7

NON-STATE ACTORS AND ENVIRONMENTAL ENFORCEMENT

In his proposal for a green criminology, Lynch (1990: 3) noted that "powerful groups manipulate and use race, class, gender and the environment to preserve the basis of their power." Social movements that represent "civil society" have drawn on these concerns to oppose the power and effects of the ToP. Criminologists, however, have paid little attention to these concerns (except see Nurse 2013; Ellefsen 2012; Myrup 2012; Stretesky *et al.* 2010). While green criminologists have neglected this issue, ToP theorists have been much more receptive to this area of study (Gould *et al.* 1996).

For green criminologists the study of social movements focused on environmental enforcement activities are critically important because they have the potential to influence state definitions and enforcement of environmental crimes, as well as normative definitions of green crime. A number of local and global non-profit organizations have taken up the fight against ecological disorganization. This chapter explores those efforts to contain ecological disorganization. We begin our analysis by drawing upon treadmill of production theory to describe how social movement or civil society organizations can advocate for environmental protection within existing local and global political economies. This advocacy focuses on changing environmental laws and the enforcement of those laws. While state actors possess the potential to prevent and control ecological disorganization, citizens' organizations may play an equally important role by pressuring the state to act on issues of public importance. In doing so, we provide some examples of this process, and explore how these issues relate to green criminology.

In addition, we draw upon the work of ToP theorists, environmental justice scholars, and green criminologists to examine the composition and distribution of local and global environmental enforcement organizations. While we are optimistic that civil society organizations have the potential to combat forms of green crime, these organizations may fail to solve environmental problems because they become part of the power structure that promotes environmental injustice and maintains treadmill policies that lead to green crime. For instance, the distribution of civil society environmental organizations across nations tends to be associated with the nation's levels of economic development (Gómez 2008). This may facilitate treadmill practices that benefit high-income nations over low-income nations with respect to international environmental policies (Gómez 2008; Smith and Wiest 2005). In this case, influential non-profit environmental organizations headquartered in high-income countries may operate in a neo-colonialist and unjust fashion (Gómez 2008). Thus, there may be an uneven geography of environmental enforcement, associated with the emergence of civil society organizations across the globe, that facilitates existing treadmill of production policies (e.g., Knight and Stretesky 2011).

Civil society, green crime and the treadmill of production

Civil society organizations (CSOs) consist of non-profit organizations that pursue democratic interests outside the scope of the governmental and economic institutions. CSOs in the environmental enforcement arena advocate for environmental protection within a political economy of production. As previously noted, the engine that drives the ToP is capitalist expansion. In that context, corporate actors focus on increasing production for profit and are driven by the bottom line and tend to promote production at the cost of environmental destruction. In many cases corporations locate in countries with the lowest wages and weakest environmental laws in order to minimize production costs associated with the extraction of natural resources. For its part, labor may be motivated to support increases in production to maintain employment and increase wages, and in this way, though perhaps unintentionally, prevent social disorganization. As ToP theorists note, consequently, labor may sometimes pursue policies that increase ecological disorganization to minimize social disorganization (Gould *et al.* 1996). Finally, as ToP treadmill theorists suggest, state actors may support the expansion of production to enhance revenues that result from tax policies to facilitate state welfare policies. Thus, tax revenues that are tied to economic production help to legitimate the role of the state (Schnaiberg 1980). As a result, the state may often support the development of ToP practices that harm the environment. As pointed out in Chapter 4, states may even lower their environmental standards to attract business.

Like treadmill theorists, criminologists should also be concerned with a fourth set of actors seeking to reduce ecological disorganization: CSOs. Generally, the state operates in the interest of treadmill actors. If, however, civil actors organize to promote ecological interests, they can sometimes influence state policies by slowing the treadmill of production and preventing green crimes. In this sense, CSOs act in opposition to corporate interests tied to expanding the ToP. In forming oppositional groups, CSOs may pressure the state to manage conflicts concerning the disorganizing effects of production on the environment (Obach 2004).

The idea that CSOs can pressure the state has relevance to green criminology with respect to the definition of environmental crime and its enforcement. For example, CSOs represent an important and external force on state actors (Boli and Thomas 1997, 1999) that enhances the commitment to actively police and prosecute environmental crimes. For his part, Schnaiberg is cautiously optimistic concerning the effect of CSOs (Gould *et al.* 1996). Based on that view, it should be noted that while citizen groups have not yet forced states to adopt steady environmental policies, CSOs provide important challenges to ecological disorganization, and can help expand the definition of environmental crime to be more consistent with a definition of green crime. There is some anecdotal evidence that supports this contention, which we explore below.

Types of environmental enforcement organizations

Environmental enforcement organizations (EEOs) are one type of CSO that engages in both advocacy and operations on a variety of scales from local to global governments. EEOs are typically non-profits, operating independently from the state. By definition, EEOs are advocates for stronger environmental laws and enforcement. At the local level, EEOs may aid in environmental monitoring for state organizations. At the international level, while often headquartered in one country, EEOs advocate in several countries. At the local and international levels EEOs may lobby, denounce, and even promote state environmental enforcement. In addition to advocating for stronger environmental policy and practices, EEOs may carry out enforcement operations such as law enforcement and prosecution functions. For instance, at the international level the Sea Shepherd Conservation Society engages in operations and "confrontational tactics due to its sophisticated use of international law, and by taking advantage of overlapping international legal regimes," in order to prevent wildlife violations (Bondaroff 2011). Similar organizations (such as Greenpeace) also engage in enforcement and monitor environmental conditions in order to shift the "balance of power between activists, state regulators, and private firms based on their ability to contest official accounts of environmental quality" with information on environmental performance (Overdevest and Mayer 2008: 1497).

While EEOs could be classified as belonging to one of two camps (advocacy or operations), in reality the distinction between advocacy and operations is not always clear, and many EEOs engage in both types of action. This is the case for other types of environmental organizations as well. For example, Gould *et al.* (2008: 104) point out that in order to challenge the ToP, EEOs "disrupt, monitor, and shame transnational corporations into behaving responsibly." If treadmill theorists are correct, then EEOs help shape the formal governmental social control of environmental harms through a variety of methods that include protest, political pressure and campaigns, campaign contributions and political support, petitions and lobbying, and actual enforcement-related efforts with state support (Burns *et al.* 2008). Thus, while Schnaiberg (1980) clearly notes that capital is the dominant actor that drives ecological disorganization, it is clear that citizen groups in the form of EEOs also have the ability to influence state actors in the environmental crime arena. In order to examine the impact of advocacy and operations organizations we will consider them carefully, noting how these groups may influence green crime at both local and international levels.

Advocacy

EEOs may serve as advocacy organizations that promote sustainable environmental laws or pressure the state into enforcing current environmental laws. Knight and Stretesky (2011: 16) define lobbying and advocacy organizations as organized actors that "advocate or lobby governments (international, national, state, or local) for the creation or enforcement of environmental laws, rules, regulations, or agreements." The Coalition for a Clean Baltic (www.ccb.se/about.html), for example, is an international non-governmental organization that "promotes the protection and improvement of the Baltic Sea environment and natural resources ... at the international and national policy levels." Its website notes that the group approaches this goal primarily through lobbying, which includes creating "public opinion about Baltic Sea issues," and through joint appeals to organizations such as the Baltic Marine Environmental Protection Commission, which creates policy for the region.

In terms of advocacy, international EEOs have gained considerable legitimacy with respect to environmental protection. The legitimacy of EEOs is strengthened because no state has authority over any other. Thus, international organizations serve an important global function and can direct the global culture with respect to important collective values. Boli and Thomas (1997: 181) suggest that international non-governmental organizations (INGOs) "cannot dominate in the conventional sense." They have "little sanctioning power, yet they act as if they were authorized in the strongest possible terms. They make rules and expect them to be followed; they plead their views with states or transnational corporations and express moral condemnation when their pleas go unheeded."

Thus, international EEOs can advocate for environmental law and influence states because they can negotiate issues of sovereignty more easily than states. Boli and Thomas (1997) point out that international EEOs are in a position to influence states' behavior even when those organizations are not engaging in environmental enforcement. Thus, EEOs may help shape the environmental crime agendas and state behavior toward environmental crime. Frank (1997) suggests that international EEOs are also significant actors in environmental sectors that can impact the way states have developed environmental policy. Thus, international EEOs may stigmatize violators and direct attention to corporate environmental destruction (Boli and Thomas 1997).

Advocacy INGOs may influence the state by pushing for greater levels of enforcement. At the local level, EEO members may attend meetings with enforcement personnel and prompt those state actors to take strong action on environmental issues that are important to the community. This effort may influence the operation of law in any particular area where these groups are located. At the local level, for example, Stretesky, Shelley, and Crow (2010) discovered that environmental organizations influence environmental enforcement across counties in Florida, USA. They found that members of environmental organizations attended meetings with enforcement personnel and discovered that enforcement personnel took their concerns seriously – especially at the local level. The number of EEOs was positively associated with environmental violations, and they hypothesized that organizations were responsible for higher levels of enforcement (Stretesky *et al.* 2010). Similar arguments have been made at the global level, where citizen activism around environmental issues has emerged as a response to global ecological troubles. As Gould, Pellow, and Schnaiberg (2008: 101) observe:

> Transnational social movement organizations are proliferating and have been since the dawn of the post-World War II era ... [Social movement organizations] are now widely acknowledged

as formidable players in international politics because they are creating new global norms and practices among states, international bodies, and corporations, and transforming new ones. Such non-state actors can be viewed as sources of resistance to globalization from below.

To be sure, international organizations that operate within the environmental arena have been able to shape and influence environmental crime across the globe.

Operations

EEOs engage in operations-related activities such as training law enforcement personnel, monitoring environmental violations, and even prosecuting environmental offenders. In some cases governments may deliver enforcement programs through non-profit organizations that operate within their countries (Srivastava *et al.* 2012). Thus, some EEOs work within the confines of existing laws to enhance environmental enforcement and to aid state law enforcement. Knight and Stretesky (2011: 15) define EEOs that engaged in operations as:

> Nonprofit organizations that carry out international, national, state, or local legal actions (civil or criminal) to enforce environmental laws, rules, regulations, or agreements and/or obtain penalties or criminal sanctions for violations. This includes monitoring efforts. Organizations may also provide direct aid (in the form of resources or monitoring for environmental violations) to state or other governmental agencies that carry out environmental protection efforts.

Consistent with this definition are international organizations that engage in monitoring practices by taking air samples in what have been described as "bucket brigades." Bucket brigades developed as citizen-led community policing efforts at the local level that sample air quality to help identify violations (O'Rourke and Macey 2003).

This form of policing is now being implemented globally. For instance, Global Community Monitor (http://gcmonitor.org/index. php) operates in more than a dozen countries (Australia, USA, Zambia, Nigeria, South Africa, Thailand, Israel, the Philippines, India, Kazakhstan, Netherlands, Ireland, England, Spain, Barbados, and Curacao) and trains community organizations in how to monitor air released from industrial facilities. Information obtained from community monitoring can aid in direct enforcement operations and influence advocacy efforts from outside.

Within the United States, Lynch and Stretesky (2013) found that the US Environmental Protection Agency relied on an extensive number of community organizations to verify water quality across the country to aid in monitoring water quality and violations. These organizations often foster a sense of community "because they want to help protect a stream, lake, bay or wetland near where they live, work, or play" (US Environmental Protection Agency 2002: 1). Thus, citizen non-profit organizations promote a focus on quality issues through the decentralization of environmental enforcement activities (US Environmental Protection Agency 2002). This notion is consistent with the idea that a new era of community-type policing has emerged, represented by a decentralization of police power (Oliver 1998). Lynch and Stretesky found that citizen water-monitoring organizations worked with state and environmental agencies by recruiting and training community members to monitor water quality to facilitate direct state action and to identify sources of pollution that impact their communities. Warchol and Kapla (2012) found that within South Africa, non-profit organizations were helping train wildlife conservation officers stationed in some wildlife parks in that country.

With respect to environmental crime, organizational constraints faced by environmental enforcement agencies make these non-governmental organizations (NGOs) critical to environmental crime reduction efforts. Citizen organizations engage in informal surveillance activities designed to identify environmental violations and can report those violations to authorities. It should come as no surprise, then, that EEOs can become part of citizen watch programs developed as part of community-oriented policing efforts (Oliver 1998), and can help identify environmental law violations when formal law-enforcement organizations lack the resources necessary to monitor local pollution problems (O'Rourke and Macey 2003). The usefulness and effect of these monitoring efforts should not be underestimated. As Overdevest and Mayer (2008: 1497) suggest, "local antitoxic organizations have realized the importance of collecting and diffusing information in order to influence industrial firms' environmental performance."

In some cases operations organizations go beyond monitoring and attempt to enforce laws through direct action. This is most likely to happen when law enforcement is not concerned with the application of environmental laws, and allows various actors to violate the law without ramifications (Bondaroff 2011). In direct enforcement operations, organizations may use the information they collect in the courts to push for compensation and punishment. For example, Earthjustice (http://earthjustice.org/about) describes itself as an organization that "works through the courts on behalf of citizen groups, scientists, and other parties to ensure government agencies and private interests follow the law." Like many environmental organizations, Earthjustice engages in lobbying-related activity. One attorney for Earthjustice suggested that for his organization:

> winning cases is often only half the battle. To keep our victories from being undone by legislative action, I often testify before the Hawaii Legislature or work with Earthjustice's policy folks in Washington, DC to influence lawmaking at the national level. I draft press releases, fact sheets, op-eds and other materials, hold press conferences, and speak at conferences to educate the press and public about the importance of our litigation efforts and to remind them about the central role environmental protection plays in improving the quality of life in Hawaii (cited in Yale Law School 2011: 19).

Some organizations fight environmental crime and deviance with illegal tactics that are labeled as "ecotage," or "monkeywrenching"

(Gottschalk 1998). These more radical, direct-action tactics are associated with groups that sometimes carry out direct action that violates the criminal law, such as Earth First! (Vanderheiden 2005). The Earth Liberation Front, for example, uses arson to stop environmental damage. One of its founder members, Rod Coranado, explains that, with respect to animals, illegal tactics are used because "after years of rescuing animals from laboratories, it was heartbreaking to see those buildings and those cages refilled within the following days. And for that reason, arson has become a necessary tool" (cited in Schorn 2005). In short, there is little doubt that environmental organizations often oppose the state and corporations through various methods and operations, but have also helped to direct the state's attention to environmental problems and issues by threatening state legitimacy. Dorn, Van Daele, and Vander Beken (2007: 23) note that NGOs "have not only provided information on otherwise neglected scandals, but also sometimes indulge in high-profile public actions – forcing the administrative and enforcement agencies to do something." Thus, these organizations have the ability to create a legitimation crisis. In the end, as citizen environmental enforcement philosophy changes, organizations will continue to develop. Some organizations will work within the system by partnering with environmental enforcement agencies, and others will work outside of the system to pressure corporations and government to modify their behavior. To date, these efforts have impacted and improved environmental quality. However, they do not appear to constrain the ToP entirely. In short, NGOs that engage in environmental enforcement and advocacy are not a panacea for changing treadmill trends or for preventing green crime. Below, we explore some of the reasons why this may be true.

Problems of justice

Environmental justice is an important issue among treadmill theorists and green criminologists (Gould *et al.* 2008; Lynch and Stretesky 2012; Huss *et al.* 2012; Stretesky *et al.* 2011; Stretesky and Lynch 2002, 1999a, 1999b; White 2008). Rhodes (2005: 8) defines environmental justice as the fair treatment of all races, cultures, incomes and education levels with respect to the development, implementation, and enforcement of environmental laws, regulations and policies. Fair treatment implies that no population of people should be forced to shoulder a disproportionate share of the negative environmental impacts of pollution or environmental hazards or be denied a proportionate share of the positive benefits of environmental regulation or program environmental hazards due to lack of political or economic strength.

Moreover, as Gould, Pellow, and Schnaiberg (2008: 22) note, "environmental problems and solutions are not distributed evenly across or within populations," meaning that it is also important to address inequality in the distribution of enforcement of environmental regulations (Lynch *et al.* 2004a 2004b). The study of environmental justice helps explain why non-governmental EEOs cannot always limit the ToP, or limit ecological disorganization and the volume of green crime. Both between and within countries we believe there is (1) a trend in the formalization of environmental enforcement organizations that prevents them from effectively challenging the political economy of ecological disorganization, and (2) an unequal distribution of enforcement organizations that prevents them from operating where problems are significant.

Formalization of organizations

Over time, organizations within a social movement sector tend to become more formalized (Benford 2005). With respect to environmental organizations in general, Robert Brulle (2000) observes that many tend to be bureaucratic in nature, relying on significant levels of external funding. Thus, it seems plausible that the formalization of EEOs may undermine their effectiveness. That is, as EEOs are formalized, they may be unable to contest state support of the treadmill in any serious fashion. For instance, Brulle and Pellow (2005) put forward the idea that a heavy reliance on foundation funding has placed environmental justice organizations in a particularly vulnerable position because they are unable to undermine the policies of their funding sources. Benford (2005) offers similar observations about the status of environmental justice organizations, and argues that, as they have formalized, they chase money and funding. In short, both Brulle (2000) and Benford (2005) contend that extensive reliance on larger and more formal organizations may decrease democratic grass-roots struggles.

The process of becoming formalized may corrupt the mission of EEOs and cause them to pursue activities to obtain funding rather than to uphold their principles. Few studies address this issue. However, in a study of environmental justice organizations in the United States, Rios (2000) found that many organizations could be described as formal interest groups as opposed to grassroots organizations. She concluded that this situation may lead to conditions where organizations are more responsive to state and corporate funders than to civil society. Thus, non-profit EEOs that operate in wealthy countries may not frame environmental protection in the same way as poor countries because funding dictates and directs priorities (Benford 2005). In order for non-profit EEOs to slow green crime they cannot be funded by corporations and be directed by state agencies. This idea has lead many environmental movements to resist formalization. The First National People of Color Environmental Leadership Summit, for example, brought together many grassroots organizations and promoted the idea that environmental justice groups must maintain their insurgent structure and avoid becoming formalized (Cole and Foster 2001). The extent to which this has actually occurred, however, may be questioned, given the number of environmental justice organizations that appear in various directories that tend to measure more formal organizations (Stretesky *et al.* 2011).

Another consequence of group formalization is that there is the strong potential for organizations to shy away from challenging production. Schelly and Stretesky (2009) provide one explanation for what consequences this might have in the environmental enforcement arena with regard to environmental justice organizations. They found that when environmental justice protests successfully prevented the siting of hazardous waste facilities in socially disadvantaged areas, those facilities simply moved to other, even more socially disadvantaged areas, where they appeared to encounter little resistance. Thus, because the focus of the protests was on distribution rather than production, the organizations involved in the protest presented no serious challenge to treadmill policies. Therefore, while some distributional protests are successful, they do not appear to place limits on ecological destruction because there is always somewhere else to pollute. For this reason, protests that focus on the distribution of waste may not limit geographic inequality or ecological destruction. Instead they may promote a path of least resistance policy on the part of the ToP.

While there is no guarantee that grassroots organizations will be free from pressure and cooptation by the state, the fact that EEOs are headquartered in high-income countries, and high-income locales within countries, raises serious questions about the development of a global civil society that can alter treadmill practices. We address the distribution of non-profit organizations next.

Distribution of organizations

Within the United States and across the globe, non-profit organizations that engage in environmental enforcement are not distributed equally, or according to the distribution of environmental problems. For instance, Lynch and Stretesky (2013) studied the distribution of locally based water-monitoring organizations in the US by drawing upon traditional social movement literature. They argue that the unequal distribution of such organizations is likely to exist because many monitoring programs require technology and human capital to be successful and are therefore likely to be dependent upon community wealth (see also Ottinger 2010). Thus, while environmental enforcement agencies may aid organizations with some costs, Lynch and Stretesky (2013) believe that EEOs are more likely to form in those enforcement regions where organizational resources for their support exists. They discovered that there is an association between traditional economic disadvantage and the distribution of water-monitoring organizations across states.

Support for this position on the distribution of EEOs has been found among studies of environmental justice organizations (see Stretesky *et al.* 2011 for a review). Within the criminology literature, Somerville (2009) makes a similar point about uneven enforcement in the case of community-oriented policing. With respect to EEOs, Frickel (2004) summarizes the problem nicely, suggesting that an unequal distribution of enforcement information has the potential to create asymmetrical relationships, where technology and information become more concentrated and available to those citizens who have resources. In short, one of the potential unintended consequences of community environmental policing is the generation of inequality in the distribution of citizen monitoring groups that can collaborate with state and federal enforcement agencies for environmental enforcement purposes. The potential unequal distribution of EEOs has two consequences. First, disadvantaged communities are less able to protect and police their communities. Second, green crimes will be more likely to occur within areas where environmental enforcement is least likely – exactly where non-governmental organizations are needed the most. These two observations are consistent with the environmental injustice literature, where it has been observed that minorities and the poor are more likely to be located in proximity to environmental hazards than whites and the more affluent (Bullard 1993).

The same processes that create the unequal distribution of EEOs within countries operate globally. For instance, the unequal distribution of international EEOs across the globe may mean that activism is directed from high-income countries to low-income countries that lack the ability to form organizations because of resource deprivation. Such a condition suggests that environmental injustice exists with respect to the benefits of global environmental regulation because of a lack of political or economic strength. Unfortunately, EEOs located in high-income countries may direct volunteers in low-income field offices that don't understand local culture (Grossman and Rangan 2000). Under such circumstances international EEOs directed from high-income countries may have trouble addressing ecological disorganization in low-income countries. McPeak (2001: 478) recognizes this problem for non-governmental organizations in general and suggests that the development of international non-governmental organizations has begun to "decentralize their management structures," and is "accompanied by increasing levels of conflict between field and headquarters staff, falling morale, and proposals to recentralize operational management."

The global distribution of non-governmental organizations may also be related to environmental justice because organizations in high-income countries may actually destabilize civil society in low-income countries. On this point, Gómez (2008: 6) notes:

> In the last years ... a number of Northern NGOs are opening offices in the South, engaging local organisations as representatives or establishing other forms of physical presence. The assumption behind it is that this would make their organisations more efficient and effective, being nearer the target group and the partners in the South. However, there are also some negative views on the move, which has been referred to as a form of neo-colonialism.

Thus, the distribution of global environmental enforcement headquarters in high-income countries may be detracting from the development of similar programs in low-income countries. Because low-income nations lack environmental enforcement headquarters, they may be less likely to form those types of organizations because they must compete with EEOs in wealthy countries for funding and resources (Stretesky et al. 2011). Low-income countries would then be in a position where environmental enforcement policing levels were based on funding directed from foundations and governments in high-income countries. Thus, the agglomeration of EEOs across the globe may shape the global distribution of community environmental policing and advocacy and allow treadmill policies to continue, increasing the level of green crime in low-income countries.

With respect to the distribution of international EEOs, Knight and Stretesky (2011) found that the per capita income for those countries without any environmental enforcement headquarters was less than half of the per capita income for those countries with at least one EEO ($5,210 vs. $13,705). That evidence is enough to raise serious questions about the distribution of EEOs across the globe.

Conclusion

The operations and advocacy aspects of EEOs should be of specific interest to green criminologists because those organizations have implications for how green criminology is put into practice. And, while EEOs have taken up a major role in the development and enforcement of environmental laws, green criminologists have not paid significant attention to EEOs. This omission is surprising because the development of civil society has significant implications for the prevention of green crime.

EEOs have the potential to limit treadmill practices because they can influence government in ways that unorganized citizens cannot, and also because they can influence corporate actors. In short, citizen-led environmental organizations that develop outside the formal state system may be in direct conflict with the state and may put considerable pressure on policy-makers and enforcement agencies.

Green criminologists interested in environmental justice should direct attention to studying the distribution of EEOs. For example, environmental injustice may occur because environmental enforcement is not evenly distributed across nations. We have raised several concerns that we believe are tied to composition and location of emerging EEOs. We caution that the potential consequences associated with the uneven development of environmental enforcement are environmental injustice and the facilitation of treadmill policies. Countries that are relatively poor will see less enforcement and fewer environmental regulations than countries that are relatively wealthy. In short, countries where INGOs are headquartered may have more environmental protection and may be determining where pockets of global environmental enforcement are directed. It is our hope that green criminologists will be encouraged to expand their research on the role of non-governmental EEOs, including the role and impact of these organizations in preventing environmental crime and ecological disorganization.

8

CONCLUSION

It is widely accepted that capitalism relies on accumulation, expressed both in the growth of capital itself and in stored labor or the commodification and transformation of labor into goods and services. In radical economics, central to this process of accumulation is the unequal ownership of the means of production and capital, the exploitation of labor, and the production of surplus value (Marx 1976 [1867]). The long-run success of capitalism depends on its ability to produce and instill a belief in its core values, especially the ideas that accumulation enhances quality of life, that through hard work anyone can succeed and obtain "the good life," and that individuals and society can benefit and improve their standard of living through consumption at both individual and social level, as mass consumption of goods and services expands. In order to justify the transformation of nature into useful commodities, capitalism stripped nature of its unity and treated it as the raw materials of production (O'Connor 1998). The capitalist view of nature excluded the possibility that "discrete things" in nature were part of a larger living organism or ought to be treated as independent, living entities with uses beyond those invented by humans. In effect, the ideology of nature produced by capitalism is based on a deconstruction of nature into isolated and abstract, discrete entities. This deconstruction of nature has paved the way for large-scale environmental destruction to facilitate the expansion of the capitalist system of production in ways that are consistent with accumulative tendencies. This is what O'Connor (1998) refers to as the philosophical dichotomy between man and nature as independent rather than related entities. In short, the expansion of accumulation, the extraction of surplus value, and economic growth and consumption drive this system.

Green criminology was developed in the 1990s to provide critical insight into the ways that capitalism can disorganize and destroy ecosystems and the biosphere (Lynch 1990). The purpose of green criminology was to foster thinking that challenges the growth assumption within capitalism, and to help modify thinking about crime, ecology, and the economy. The challenge of green criminology has not yet been realized. We believe that green criminologists have not identified its core concerns, laid out an agreement about its primary theoretical orientations and allegiances, or precisely defined its key theoretical concepts. This lack of clarity about the scope, purpose, and theoretical orientation of green criminology proves difficult when it comes to identifying the kinds of crimes and harms that ought to be included as legitimate subject matter within the discipline. A simple way to address this challenge would be to assert that green criminology is a legitimate mechanism for studying all forms of harm that may be related to the environment. This approach, we believe, would transform green criminology into an area of study. From our point of view, however, this is undesirable. Instead, since green criminology was originally conceived as being centered in the political economic analysis of environmental harms, crimes, law, and justice, it is necessary for those who wish to take a different view to justify their position and to explain why their view is more fitting or appropriate than a green criminology situated in radical political economy.

Recently, green criminology has been examined from a cultural, organizational, and even "personal troubles" approach (Mills 1959). As we have argued, green crimes are more than personal troubles – they are public, and patterned by and extensively connected to the economy and the ecology. To demonstrate this point we have focused on ToP theory (Schnaiberg 1980). When ToP is used as a framework for organizing green criminology, we begin to see that green crimes can be boiled down to crimes that are a result of ecological withdrawals and those that are a result of ecological additions. We propose that green crime should be organized in this fashion because withdrawals and additions present a language that focuses attention on the relationship between the economy and the ecology. In Chapter 3 we demonstrated how green crimes occur when natural resources are extracted from the environment, while in Chapter 4 we established that green crime occurs when pollution is released into the environment. In both cases, these green crimes were referenced to production. In short, it is our intention that green criminology be organized around the relationship between the ecology and the economy.

The ToP approach developed by Schnaiberg (1980) is heavily rooted in a political economy of the environment. This is important because the study of political economy has implications for the way natural production, ecological disorganization, and environmental destruction are treated by the state. We have pointed out that acts central to production will tend to take legal precedent over those central to ecology. And throughout this work we have demonstrated that when the state defines some acts as environmental crime it leaves out a great deal of significant ecological destruction that occurs through routine economic activity within a capitalist system. We have presented a definition of green crime that suggests that it is an act or acts that cause or have the potential to cause significant harm to ecological systems for the purposes of increasing or supporting economic production. This definition of green crime is, as we have suggested, important for green criminologists to consider if we wish to advocate for policies that will do something about the rising ecological threats.

Ecosystems can be irreparably destroyed even when environmental laws are strictly adhered to. It is this ecosystem harm and the general acceleration of the ToP that criminologists should be concerned with studying. We believe that criminologists who study environmental crime but ignore ecosystem disorganization and disruption are simply engaging in the task of "rearranging deckchairs on the Titanic." The task of greening criminology, then, is futile if the relationship between the ecology and the economy is not considered central to the analysis. But how should green criminologists proceed? We offer some suggestions for future study that focus more centrally on the relationship between the economy and the ecology. We concentrate on green crime, but note that ToP has implications for the study of social disorganization, animal harm, and environmental justice.

The future of green crime

In Chapters 3 and 4 we proposed that green criminologists identify those situations where production is central to the economy, and then examine how economic production is prioritized over ecological production. As green criminologists go about answering these questions they can collaborate with natural scientists as well as engage with the scientific literature. In doing so, green criminologists can help to organize this literature, which often appears fragmented. Out of context, many studies of the natural environment provide only a limited picture of the relationship between various types of ecological damage and the common source of that damage. By drawing upon scientific studies of the environment, criminologists can organize those studies to reveal the damage to primary production units in nature, as well as to the actors and structures involved in that disruption. Criminologists can examine the potential long-term impact of the harm created and make comparisons to more orthodox crimes and punishment to reveal important contradictions in the way society treats various types of harm. Such an approach, however, will mean that green criminologists will also need to focus considerable attention on corporate, state, labor, and civil society actors.

As previously noted, corporate actors have an incentive to constantly increase production in a capitalist system, and it is often the case that the harm that production causes is hidden by ideological baggage and bias. We have demonstrated that corporations engage in acts that damage ecological systems, despite corporate and state claims that corporations have become "green." Criminologists, then, should study how corporations are able to work within the current capitalist system to manipulate laws that favor their economic interests over the interests of the ecology. We believe that green criminologists can point out those contradictions between the economy and the ecology, in order to bring attention to the issue of environmental harm. This attention has the ability to move society in positive ways, by helping to promote alternatives such as sustainable steady state economic policies. These policies are important for future generations, so that they can rely on a healthy ecosystem for their survival.

One example of this type of work is the study of the relationship between state and non-state actors and how powerful treadmill actors use their economic power to shape the law by lobbying and monetary donations. In short, laws that govern ecological additions and withdrawals may be linked to trends in corporate and state behavior. We have noted that the relationship between the state and corporations that is examined in ToP theory is readily connected to the notion of state-corporate crime as developed by Michalowski and Kramer (2007). More specifically, Michalowski and Kramer's ideas about state-facilitated crime are highly compatible with the notion of green crime and ToP because they can be applied to the study of governmental regulatory systems and the failure of laws to address ecological harm. Green criminologists can draw on the notion of state-corporate crime and do not need to rely on state definitions of crime to conduct analyses. Moreover, green criminologists can focus on how and why laws and a regulatory structure emerge that fail to prevent ecological harm. Connections that are identified in the state-corporate crime literature, then, are central in better establishing a political economy of green crime. This demonstration of how state-facilitated actions on the part of corporations are a form of crime, reframes ecological disorganization in terms that reveal the source and extent of the damage and harm that is associated with the continual expansion of production.

We argue that green criminologists should focus their research on labor and non-governmental actors to examine the role that these actors play in green crime and the definition of crime. Both labor and NGO actors have the potential to act as anti-treadmill forces that can reduce green crime and change society through their influence on governance practices. While labor can actively oppose progressive environmental policies when they believe it will hamper economic growth, this does not have to be the case, as Gould, Schnaiberg, and Weinberg (1996) point out. Environmental movement organizations can be composed of both labor and environmentalists and may be thought of as "red-green movements." In the view of red-greens, the world system of capitalism understands and treats nature as a warehouse of natural resources, to be used by humans for productive purposes (Burkett 2007; Foster 2002). That is to say, capitalism treats nature as so much or so many use values, rather than as a complex, independent, and necessary living system that other species depend upon for survival (Lovelock 2007). In the capitalist view of the world, nature has value only to the extent that it may be transformed into use values (O'Connor 1998: 21).

Importantly, while an organized civil society will likely be required to decelerate the treadmill, environmental enforcement organizations will likely play an important role in that process, because they both monitor crime and lend resources in the form of human capital needed to protect the ecosystem. Green criminologists may want to determine the conditions under which these non-government environmental enforcement organizations emerge and operate. They may ask why some environmental organizations have become successful at stopping a particular type of green crime. The success of certain organizations with respect to particular ecosystems or ecosystem components needs to be replicated across the biosphere because, as we have shown, ecological disorganization continues to increase despite the fact that there appears to be a greater awareness about environmental problems.

In addition, researchers interested in civil society need to study the problems inherent in non-governmental organizations. For instance, if environmental enforcement organizations become too reliant on state support, will they simply adopt state definitions of environmental crime? There are many reasons why this might be the case, including a basic desire to continue the organization, and we suggested in Chapter 7 that this might be so. Moreover, as we pointed out, the potential for EEOs to compete with each other for scarce resources and funding may serve to limit the number of EEOs that can emerge in any formalized fashion. This constraint means that green criminologists might focus more on grassroots organizations in order to determine how ecological disorganization will be successfully prevented. It is clear that current efforts are not enough, since ecological destruction appears to be increasing rather than decreasing.

The state reaction to environmental challenges on the part of these organizations should also be examined. As non-governmental organizations challenge the state and its enforcement practices, they will likely come under scrutiny. Organizations that operate on their own definitions of green crime – those that are not accepted by the state – are likely to violate state laws, especially when they disrupt production. These non-state actors and the role of civil society in defining green crime remain largely understudied by green criminologists, particularly those that work in the West.

Social disorganization and animal abuse

As noted, the lack of clarity about the scope, purpose, and theoretical orientation of green criminology proves problematic when it comes to identifying the kinds of crimes and harms that ought to be included as legitimate subject matter within the discipline of green criminology. We have tackled this issue by looking at social disorganization and animal abuse. While these areas of study do not fall directly under green criminology and our definition of green crime, they are related to green criminology; and, as we have argued, they are important areas of study and can help shed light on the relationship between the ecology and the economy. With respect to ecological disorganization, we find that the treadmill not only creates surplus labor through the use of chemical technology that facilitates production, it also impacts the way people live, work, and play in communities across the globe. For instance, when massive ecological withdrawals occur in a community, those withdrawals can disrupt sustainable economies and lead to serious social disorganization. Moreover, as resources are quickly extracted from the ecology, people living near those resources are likely to feel the social consequences because of what some theorists call the "natural resource curse." As we demonstrated in Chapter 5, natural resource extraction and social disorganization often go hand in hand. Production-related pollution might also facilitate social disorganization and crime when substances are released into the environment that may alter behavior in entire communities. Green criminologists should examine this issue as outcomes of the ecology–economy relationship. Moreover, criminologists in general would do well to focus on the relationship between the economy and ecology when examining various forms and types of crimes across the globe.

We also demonstrated why animal abuse should be important to green criminologists. While at first glance a significant amount of animal abuse may not appear to fit under the definition of green crime, we have shown that there is a connection. Some forms of animal abuse occur when animals become victims of the treadmill and their natural spaces are turned into human habitats. Animals, like humans, are also impacted by pollution in the form of toxic waste releases, spills, and disposal. In addition, if certain types of wild animals become valuable consumption targets, they may be completely removed as actors in an ecosystem, which not only harms the animals but disrupts the ecosystems from which they were removed. In short, we have demonstrated that there is strong reason to include animal abuse as an area of concern for green criminologists.

Green victims and environmental justice

As Lynch and Stretesky (2003) argue, the "meaning of green" is critically important within criminology. The definition of green is critical to future studies within the field of green crime. If we apply the state's definition of crime to environmental crime, entire groups of victims are ignored. As such, a variety of green crime victims suffer serious harm but have not received sufficient attention in the criminological literature. We believe that this is an issue of environmental injustice. From a treadmill perspective, the search for inexpensive raw materials and labor continually shifts the balance of the world marketplace of capitalism. This shifting pattern of global resource extraction, consumption, accumulation, and labor can be stabilized through unequal relationships between the core capitalist nations (those with elevated standards of living, commodity consumption, and ownership of capital and production) and peripheral nations where the costs of labor are low and raw materials plentiful. This environmental injustice is inherent in the ToP and green crime. This is also why criminologists around the world need to be engaged in a political economy of green crime.

We suggest that much more needs to be done to identify those victims who are impacted by production through environmental additions and withdrawals because of their relationship with the environment, and view this as an important direction for green criminology. While we recognize that some people may suggest that victims can choose to live different lives or live in different locales where they will not be impacted by ecological disruption, we have argued that this is simply not possible because the harms associated with production are too widespread to avoid. To be sure, green victimization is the price people pay for their modern way of life. However, that does not mean that they choose to be victims of ecological disorganization, or that they understand the current extent or causes of their victimization.

Unequal green victimization has yet to be adequately discussed and studied in the criminology literature, even though there has been some attention to the unequal distribution of environmental hazards. The problem of green victimization is one of economics, and more specifically the political economy of capitalism as it now plays out in the world capitalist system, and within nations relative to "localized" or national political economic structures. At both the world systems level and the national political economic level, the quest for profit and the obsession with accumulation and "improved" economic standards of living, the expansion of inequality in the distribution of ownership and wealth or class relations, and the ToP, all play significant roles in ecological destruction, green victimization, and environmental injustice.

In sum

For capitalism to grow, it must stimulate demand for commodities and seek out raw materials and inexpensive labor. Some might doubt that capitalism drives environmental destruction, but those who do are probably unaware of the historical relationship between capital and the environment. For capital, nature is nothing more than a warehouse of raw materials to be exploited in the pursuit of profit (Burkett 2007). Capital does not tally the costs of the damage it produces as part of any of its ledgers of production, nor does it possess the long-run vision or the ability to step outside of its present-oriented self-interest that drives profit-making to consider the needs of future generations. Capital is a hedonistic, self-interested system of production and consumption based on expansion, and at every step throughout its life course it has offended against nature.

To be sure, there are those who argue that the state and civil society can slow the increasing and harmful extraction of natural resources. However, capital interests are able to shape the laws so that extraction continues at an increasing rate. This increasing rate of natural resource extraction undoes nature, and in so doing generates unsustainable rates of environmental disorganization through the release of pollution into the environment. As we have noted, the study of these processes is not only important, but, we believe, the future of criminology.

REFERENCES

Agnew, R. (1998) "The causes of animal abuse: A social-psychological analysis," *Theoretical Criminology*, 2, 2: 177–209.

Agnew, R. (2011) "The ordinary acts that contribute to ecocide: A criminological analysis," paper presented at the American Society of Criminology, Washington, DC, November.

Agnew, R. (2012) "Dire forecast: A theoretical model of the impact of climate change on crime," *Theoretical Criminology*, 16: 21–42.

Akcil, A. and Koldas, S. (2006) "Acid mine drainage (AMD): Causes, treatment and case studies," *Journal of Cleaner Production*, 14: 1139–45.

Akers, R.L. (2009) *Social Learning and Social Structure: A General Theory of Crime and Deviance*, New Brunswick, NJ: Transaction.

Alaca, E. and George, A. (2008) "Wildlife across our borders: A review of the illegal trade in Australia," *Australian Journal of Forensic Sciences*, 40: 147–60.

Allison, E.H., Perry, A.L., Badjeck, M.C., Adger, W.N., Brown, K., Conway, D., Halls, A.S., Pilling, G.M., Reynolds, J.D., Andrew, N.L. and Dulvy, N.K. (2009) "Vulnerability of national economies to the impacts of climate change on fisheries," *Fish and Fisheries*, 10: 173–96.

Andresen, M.A. (2012) "Unemployment and crime: A neighborhood level panel data approach," *Social Science Research*, 41: 1615–28.

Andrews, A. (2009) *Unconventional Gas Shales: Development, Technology, and Policy Issues*, CRS Report R40894. Congressional Research Service. Available at <www.fas.org/sgp/crs/misc/R40894.pdf> (accessed 29 April 2013).

Appelbaum, R.P. and Christerson, B. (1997) "Cheap labor strategies and export – oriented industrialization: Some lessons from the Los Angeles/ East Asia apparel connection," *International Journal of Urban and Regional Research*, 21: 202–17.

Arluke, A., Levin, J., Luke, C. and Ascione, F. (1999) "The relationship of animal abuse and other forms of antisocial behavior," *Journal of Interpersonal Violence*, 14, 9: 963–75.

Arrhenius, S. (1908) *Worlds in the Making: The Evolution of the Universe*. New York, NY: Harper and Brothers.

Ashton, T.S. (1924) *Iron and Steel in the Industrial Revolution*. Manchester: Manchester University Press.

Bailey, W.C., Martin, J.D. and Gray, L.N. (1974) "Crime and deterrence: A correlation analysis," *Journal of Research in Crime and Delinquency*, 11, 2: 124–43.

Bandura, A. (1986) *Social Foundations of Thought and Action: A Social Cognitive Theory*. Englewood Cliffs, NJ: Prentice-Hall.

Bannon, I. and Collier, P. (2003) *Natural Resources and Violent Conflicts*. Washington, DC: World Bank.

Barraza, L. and Walford, R.A. (2002) "Environmental education: A comparison between English and Mexican school children," *Environmental Education Research*, 8, 2: 171–86.

Becker, G.S. (1968) "Crime and punishment: An economic approach," *Journal of Political Economy*, 76: 169–217.

Beckwith, R. (2010) "Hydraulic fracturing: The fuss, the facts, the future," *Journal of Petroleum Technology*, 62: 34–41.

Beder, S. (2001) "Global spin," in R. Starkey and R. Welford (eds) *Earthscan Reader in Business and Sustainable Development*. London: Earthscan.

Beirne, P. (1999) "For a nonspeciesist criminology: Animal abuse as an object of study," *Criminology*, 37, 1: 117–48.

Beirne, P. (2007) *Confronting Animal Abuse: Law, Criminology and Human-Animal Relations*. Lanham, MD: Rowman and Littlefield.

Benford, R. (2005) "The half-life of the environmental justice frame: Innovation, diffusion, and stagnation," in D.N. Pellow and R. Brulle (eds) *Power, Justice, and the Environment: A Critical Appraisal of the Environmental Justice Movement*. Cambridge, MA: MIT.

Benton, T. (1998) "Rights and justice on a shared planet: More rights or new relations?" *Theoretical Criminology*, 2, 2: 149–75.

Bodkin, J.L., Ballachey, B.E., Coletti, H.A., Esslinger, G.G., Kloecker, K.A., Rice, S.D., Reed, J.A. and Monson, D.H. (2012) "Long-term effects of the *Exxon Valdez* oil spill: Sea otter foraging in the intertidal as a pathway of exposure to lingering oil," *Marine Ecology Progress Series*, 447: 273–87.

Boli, J. and Thomas, G.M. (1997) "World culture in the world polity: A century of international non-governmental organization," *American Sociological Review*, 62, 2: 171–90.

Boli, J. and Thomas, G.M. (1999) *Organizations since 1875*. Stanford, CA: Stanford University Press.

Bondaroff, T. (2011) "Sailing with the Sea Shepherds," *Journal of Military and Strategic Studies*, 13, 3: 1–55.

Bonds, E. (2007) "Environmental review as battleground: Corporate power, government collusion, and citizen opposition to a tire-burning power plant in rural Minnesota, USA," *Organization and Environment*, 20, 2: 157–76.

Bonnell, T.R., Reyna-Hurtado, R. and Chapman, C.A. (2011) "Post-logging recovery time is longer than expected in an East African tropical forest," *Forest Ecology and Management*, 261, 4: 855–64.

Botting, J.H. and Morrison, A.R. (1993) "Animal research is vital to medicine," *Scientific American*, 276, 2: 83–5.

Boyce, J.K. (2002) *The Political Economy of the Environment*. Cheltenham: Edward Elgar.

Brauer, J. (2011) *War and Nature. The Environmental Consequences of War in a Globalized World*. Lanham, MD: AltaMira.

Brisman, A. (2008) "Crime–environment relationship and environmental justice," *Seattle Journal for Social Justice*, 6: 1–51.

British Petroleum, Inc. (2011) *BP Statistical Review of World Energy*. Online. Available at <www.bp.com/statisticalreview> (accessed 29 July 2012).

Brommer, J.E. and Møller, A.P. (2010) "Range margins, climate change, and ecology," in A.P. Møller, F. Wolfgang and P. Berthold (eds) *Effects of Climate Change on Birds*. New York, NY: Oxford.

Bronen, R. (2009) "Forced migration of Alaskan indigenous communities due to climate change: Creating a human rights response," in A. Oliver-Smith and X. Shen (eds) *Linking Environmental Change, Migration and Social Vulnerability*. Bonn, Germany: Institute for Environment and Human Security.

Brown, P., Zavestoski, S., McCormick, S., Mayer, B., Morello-Frosch, R. and Altman, R.G. (2004) "Embodied health movements: New approaches to social movements in health," *Sociology of Health and Illness*, 26, 1: 50–80.

Brulle, R. (2000) *Agency, Democracy, and Nature*. Cambridge, MA: MIT.

Brulle, R.J. and Pellow, D.N. (2005) *Power, Justice and the Environment: A Critical Appraisal of the Environmental Justice Movement*. Cambridge, MA: MIT.

Brulle, R.J. and Pellow, D.N. (2006) "Environmental justice: Human health and environmental inequalities," *Annual Review of Public Health*, 27, 103–24.

Bullard, R. (1993) *Confronting Environmental Racism: Voices from the Grassroots*. Boston, MA: South End Press.

Bunker, S.G. (2005) "How ecologically uneven development puts the spin on the ToP," *Organization and Environment*, 18, 1: 38–54.

Burgherr, P. (2007) "In-depth analysis of accidental oil spills from tankers in the context of global spill trends from all sources," *Journal of Hazardous Materials*, 140: 245–56.

Burkett, P. (2007) *Marxism and Ecological Economics: Toward a Red and Green Political Economy*. Chicago, IL: Haymarket Books.

Burns, R.G., Lynch, M.J. and Stretesky, P.B. (2008) *Environmental Law, Crime and Justice*. El Paso, TX: LFB Scholarly Publishing.

Buttel, F.H. (2004) "ToP: An appreciation, assessment, and agenda for research," *Organization and Environment*, 1, 3: 323–36.

Cable, S. and Benson, M. (1993) "Acting locally: Environmental injustice and the emergence of grass-roots environmental organizations," *Social Problems*, 40: 464–77.

Cáceres, C. (2007) "Economical and environmental factors in light alloys automotive applications," *Metallurgical and Materials Transactions A*, 38, 7: 1649–62.

Camarero, L., Rogora, M., Mosello, R., Anderson, N.J., Barbieri, A., Botev, I., Kernan, M., Kopa, J., Korhola, A., Lotter, A., Muri, G., Postolache, C, Stuchlik, E., Thies, H.L. and Wright, R.F. (2009) "Regionalisation of chemical variability in European mountain lakes," *Freshwater Biology*, 54, 12: 2452–69.

Cantor, D. and Land, K.C. (1985) "Unemployment and crime rates in the post-World War II United States: A theoretical and empirical analysis," *American Sociological Review*, 50: 317–32.

Carrington, K., Hogg, R. and McIntosh, A. (2011) "The resource boom's underbelly: Criminological impacts of mining development," *Australian and New Zealand Journal of Criminology*, 44, 3: 335–54.

Chambliss, W.J. (1988) *Exploring Criminology*. New York: Macmillan.

Chambliss, W.J. and Seidman, R. (1982) *Law, Order, and Power*. Reading, MA: Addison-Wesley.

Charman, K. (2010) "Trashing the planet for natural gas: Shale gas development threatens freshwater sources, likely escalates climate destabilization," *Capitalism Nature Socialism*, 21, 4: 72–82.

Chiricos, T.G. (1987) "Rates of crime and unemployment: An analysis of aggregate research evidence," *Social Problems*, 34, 2: 187–212.

Clarke, R.V. (1983) "Situational crime prevention: Its theoretical basis and practical scope," *Crime and Justice: An Annual Review of Research*, 4: 225–56.

Clifford, M. and Edwards, T.D. (2012) *Environmental Crime*. Burlington, MA: Jones and Bartlett.

Cohen, L.E. and Felson, M. (1979) "Social change and crime rate trends: A routine activity approach," *American Sociological Review*, 44, 4: 588–608.

Colborn, T., Dumanoski, D. and Myers, J.P. (1996) *Our Stolen Future: Are We Threatening Our Fertility, Intelligence, and Survival? A Scientific Detective Story*. New York, NY: Dutton.

Cole, L.W. and Foster, S.R. (2001) *From the Ground Up: Environmental Racism and the Rise of the Environmental Justice Movement*. New York: NYU Press.

Cole, M.A. (2004) "Trade, the pollution haven hypothesis and the environmental Kuznets curve: Examining the linkages," *Ecological Economics*, 48: 71–81.

Connolly, G. and Burns, R.J. (1990) "Efficacy of compound 1080 livestock protection collars for killing coyotes that attack sheep," *Proceedings of the Fourteenth Vertebrate Pest Conference 1990*. Online. Available at <http://digitalcommons.unl.edu/vpc14/16> (accessed 15 January 2013).

Cornell, S. (2012) "On the system properties of the planetary boundaries," *Ecology and Society*, 17, 1: r2.

Cornish, D.B. and Clarke, R.V. (1987) "Understanding crime displacement: An application of rational choice theory," *Criminology*, 25, 4: 933–48.

Corsolini, S., Covaci, A., Ademollo, N., Focardi, S. and Schepens, P. (2006) "Occurrence of organochlorine pesticides (OCPs) and their enantiomeric signatures, and concentrations of polybrominated diphenyl ethers (PBDEs) in the Adelie penguin food web, Antarctica," *Environmental Pollution*, 140, 2: 371–82.

Couceiro, S., Hamada, N., Forsberg, B.R. and Padovesi-Fonseca, C. (2010) "Effects of anthropogenic silt on aquatic macroinvertebrates and abiotic variables in streams in the Brazilian Amazon," *Journal of Soils and Sediments* 10, 1: 89–103.

Cray, D. (2010) "Deep underground, miles of hidden wildfires rage," *Time Magazine*. Online. Available at <www.time.com/time/health/article/0,8599,2006195,00.html> (accessed 4 November 2012).

Cronin, J. and Kennedy, R. (1999) *The Riverkeepers: Two Activists Fight to Reclaim Our Environment as a Basic Human Right*. New York: Touchstone.

Crowley, T.J. (2000) "Causes of climate change over the past 1000 years," *Science*, 289, 5477: 270–7.

Crutzen, P.J. and Stoermer, E.F. (2000) *Global Change Newsletter*, 41: 17–18.

DARA (2012) *Climate Vulnerability Monitor*. Madrid, Spain: Fundacion DARA Internacional.

Difiglio, C. and Fulton, L. (2000) "How to reduce US automobile greenhouse gas emissions," *Energy*, 25: 657–73.

Dorn, N., Van Daele, S. and Vander Beken, T. (2007) "Reducing vulnerabilities to crime of the European waste management industry: The research base and the prospects for policy," *European Journal of Crime, Criminal Law and Criminal Justice*, 15: 23–36.

Downey, L., Bonds, E. and Clark, K. (2010) "Natural resource extraction, armed violence, and environmental degradation," *Organization and Environment*, 23, 4: 417–45.

Du Bois, K.E. (1997) "The illegal trade in endangered species," *African Security Review*, 6, 1: 28–41.

Economy, E. (2004) *The River Runs Black: The Environmental Challenge to China's Future*. New York: Cornell University Press.

Editorial Board (2008) "Global prospects for coal-industry development," *Coke and Chemistry*, 51, 3: 110–14.

Edwards, S.M., Edwards, T.D. and Fields, C.B. (1996) *Environmental Crime and Criminality: Theoretical and Practical Issues*. New York: Garland.

Egilman, D.S. and Bohme, R. (2005) "Over a barrel: Corporate corruption of science and its effects on workers and the environment," *International Journal of Occupational and Environmental Health*, 11, 4: 331–7.

Ehrlich, P.R. and Ehrlich, A.H. (1998) *Betrayal of Science and Reason: How Anti-Environmental Rhetoric Threatens our Future*. Washington, DC: Island Press.

Elberling, B., Sondergaard, J., Jensen, L.A., Schmidt, L.B., Hansen, B.U., Asmund, G., Zunic, T.B., Hollesen, J., Hanson, S., Jansson, P.E. and Friborg, T. (2007) "Arctic vegetation damage by winter-generated coal mining pollution released upon thawing," *Environmental Science and Technology*, 41, 7: 2407–13.

Ellefsen, R. (2012) "Green movements as threats to order and economy: Animal activists repressed in Austria and beyond," in R. Ellefsen, R. Sollund and G. Larsen (eds) *Eco-global Crimes: Contemporary Problems and Future Challenges*. London: Ashgate.

Ellefsen, R., Sollund, R. and Larsen, G. (eds) (2012) *Eco-global Crimes: Contemporary Problems and Future Challenges*. London: Ashgate.

Elliott, C. (1996) "Paradigms of forest conservation," *Unasylva*, 187, 47: 3–9.

Eman, K., Meško, G. and Fields, C.B. (2009) "Crimes against the environment: Green criminology and research challenges in Slovenia," *Journal of Criminal Justice and Security*, 11, 4: 574–92.

Erikson, K. (1978) *Everything in its Path: Destruction of Community in the Buffalo Creek Flood*. New York, NY: Simon and Schuster.

Esty, D.C. (1996) *Stepping up to the Global Environmental Challenge*. Faculty Scholarship Series, paper 449. Online. Available at <http://digitalcommons. law.yale.edu/fss_papers/449> (accessed 4 November 2012).

Fagin, D. and Lavelle, M. (1996) *Toxic Deception: How the Chemical Industry Manipulates Science, Bends the Law, and Endangers Your Health*. Secaucus, NJ: Birch Lane Press.

Fankhauser, S. (1994) "The social costs of greenhouse gas emissions: An expected value approach," *Energy Journal*, 15, 2: 157–84.

Farber, D.A. (1992) "Politics and procedure in environmental law," *Journal of Law, Economics and Organization*, 8: 59–81.

Finkel, M. and Law, A. (2011) "The rush to drill for natural gas: A public health cautionary tale," *American Journal of Public Health*, 101, 5: 784–85.

Fisher, P.B. (2011) "Climate change and human security in Tuvalu," *Global Change, Peace and Security*, 23, 3: 293–313.

Flynn, C.P. (1999) "Animal abuse in childhood and later support for interpersonal violence in families," *Society and Animals*, 7, 2: 161–72.

Flynn, L. (2005) "Poor nations are littered with old PCs, report says," *New York Times*. Online. Available at <www.nytimes.com/2005/10/24/technology/24junk.html> (accessed 1 October 2011).

Fogleman, V.M. (1989) "American attitudes towards wolves: A history of misperception," *Environmental History Review*, 13, 1: 63–94.

Food and Agriculture Organization of the United Nations (2012) *State of the World's Forests, 2012*. Italy, Rome. Online. Available at <www.fao.org/docrep/016/i3010e/i3010e.pdf> (accessed 4 November 2012).

Forbes, V.E. and Forbes, T.L. (1994) *Ecotoxicology in Theory and Practice*. New York: Chapman and Hall.

Foster, J.B. (2002) *Ecology Against Capitalism*. New York: Monthly Review Press.

Foster, J.B. (2005) "The treadmill of accumulation: Schnaiberg's environment and Marxian political economy," *Organization and Environment*, 18, 1: 7–18.

Foster, J.B. (2011) "Capitalism and the accumulation of catastrophe," *Monthly Review*, 63, 7: 1–17.

Foster, J.B., Clark, B. and York, R. (2010) *The Ecological Rift: Capitalism's War on the Earth*. New York: NYU Press.

Fourier, J.B. (1878) *The Analytical Theory of Heat*. The University Press.

Fox, N. (1995) "The inadequate protection of animals against cruel animal husbandry practices under United States law," *Whittier Law Review*, 17: 145–52.

Frank, D.J. (1997) "Science, nature, and the globalization of the environment, 1870–1990," *Social Forces*, 76, 2: 409–35.

Franz, A. (2010) "Crimes against water: The Rivers and Harbors Act of 1899," *Tulane Environmental Law Journal*, 23: 255–78.

Freeman, A.M. (2000) "Economics, incentives, and environmental regulation," in M. Kraft and N. Vig (eds) *Environmental Policy: New Directions for the Twenty-First Century*. Washington, DC: CQ Press.

Freese, B. (2003) *Coal: A Human History*. Perseus Publishing.

Frickel, S. (2004) "Just science? Organizing scientist activism in the US environmental justice movement," *Science as Culture*, 13: 449–69.

Friedrichs, D. (1996) *Trusted Criminals*. Belmont, CA: Wadsworth.

Fuschino, J. (2007) "Mountaintop coal mining and the Clean Water Act: The fight over Nationwide Permit 21," *Boston College Environmental Affairs Law Review*, 34: 179–206.

Gerken, J. (2012) "Environmental killings report reveals startling number of activist deaths," *Huffington Post*. Online. Available at <www.huffingtonpost. com/2012/06/20/environmental-killings-report_n_1605446.html> (accessed 10 August 2012).

Ghosh, T.K. and Prelas, M.A. (2009) *Energy Resources and Systems: Vol. 1, Fundamentals of Non-Renewable Resources*. Netherlands: Springer.

Gibbs, C., Gore, M., McGarrell, E. and Rivers, L. (2010) "Introducing conservation criminology: Towards interdisciplinary scholarship on environmental crimes and risks," *British Journal of Criminology*, 50, 1: 124–44.

Gibbs, L.M. (1995) *Dying From Dioxin*. Boston, MA: South End.

Gibbs, L.M. (1997) *Taking Action in Your Community, Caroline Werner Gannett Lecture Series*, Rochester, NY: Rochester Institute of Technology (18 September 1997).

Glantz, S.A., Slade, J., Bero, L.A., Hanauer, P. and Barnes, D.E. (1998) *The Cigarette Papers*. Los Angeles, CA: UC Press.

Global Footprint Network (2012a) *World Footprint*. Online. Available at <www.footprintnetwork.org/en/index.php/GFN/page/world_ footprint/> (accessed 10 August 2012).

Global Footprint Network (2012b) *Data and Results*. Online. Available at <www.footprintnetwork.org/en/index.php/GFN/page/footprint_ data_and_results> (accessed 10 August 2012).

Global Witness (2002) *Logs of War: The Timber Trade and Armed Conflict*. Programme for the International Co-operation and Conflict Resolution Fafo-report 379. Online. Available at <www.unglobalcompact.org/docs/issues_doc/ Peace_and_Business/Logs_of_War.pdf> (accessed 4 November 2012).

Global Witness (2007) *Cambodia's Family Trees: Illegal Logging and the Stripping of Public Assets by Cambodia's Elite*. Online. Available at <www.globalwitness. org/sites/default/files/pdfs/cambodias_family_trees_low_res.pdf> (accessed 10 August 2012).

Gomes, G., Meneghetti, F. and Encarnarcao, F. (2012) "The environmental impact on air quality and exposure to carbon monoxide from charcoal production in southern Brazil," *Environmental Research*, 116: 136–9.

Gómez, G.M. (2008) *Field Presence of Dutch NGOs: What is the Impact on Civil Societies in the South?* Institute of Social Studies. Online. Available at

<www.pso.nl/files/2008%20%20field%20presence%20dutch%20ngos. pdf> (accessed 12 January 2012).

Goodell, J. (2006) *Big Coal: The Dirty Secret behind America's Energy Future.* Boston, MA: Houghton Mifflin.

Gordon, D.M. (1973) "Capitalism, class, and crime in America," *Crime and Delinquency*, 19, 2: 163–86.

Gottfredson, M. and Hirschi, T. (1990) *A General Theory of Crime.* Oakland, CA: Stanford University Press.

Gottfried, M., Pauli, H., Futschik, A., Akhalkatsi, M., Barančok, P., Alonso, J.L. Coldea, G., Dick, J., Erschbamer, B., Rosa, M., Calzado, F., Kazakis, G., Krajci, J., Larsson, P., Mallaun, M., Michelsen, O., Molseev, D., Molseev, P., Molau, U., Merzouki, A., Nagy, L., Nakhutsrishvill, G., Pedersen, B., Pelino, G., Puscas, M., Rossi, G., Stanisci, A., Theurillat, J., Tomaselli, M., Villar, L., Vittoz, P., Voglatzakis, I. and Grabherr, G. (2012) "Continent-wide response of mountain vegetation to climate change," *Nature Climate Change*, 2, 2: 111–15.

Gottschalk, M. (1999) "Monkeywrenching as punishment?" *Criminal Justice Policy Review*, 10: 193–211.

Gould, K.A., Schnaiberg, A. and Weinberg, A.S. (1996) *Local Environmental Struggles: Citizen Activism in the ToP.* Cambridge: Cambridge University Press.

Gould, K.A., Pellow, D. and Schnaiberg, A. (2008) *The ToP: Injustice and Unsustainability in the Global Economy.* Boulder, CO: Paradigm.

Gray, W.B. and Shimshack, J.P. (2011) "The effectiveness of environmental monitoring and enforcement: A review of the empirical evidence," *Review of Environmental Economics and Policy*, 5, 1: 3–24.

Green, P., Ward, T. and McConnachie, K. (2007) "Logging and legality: Environmental crime, civil society and the state," *Social Justice*, 34, 2: 94–110.

Greene, J.L. and Siegel, W.C. (1994) *The Status and Impact of State and Local Regulation on Private Timber Supply.* General Technical Report RM–255. Fort Collins, CO: US Department of Agriculture, Forest Service, Rocky Mountain Forest and Range Experiment Station.

Greer, J. and Bruno, K. (1996) *Greenwash: The Reality Behind Corporate Environmentalism.* Penang, Malaysia: Third World Network.

Greider, W. (1998) *One World, Ready or Not: The Manic Logic of Global Capitalism.* New York, NY: Simon and Schuster.

Griffin, J., Duncan, R.C., Riggan, W.B. and Pellom, A.C. (1989) "Cancer mortality in US counties with hazardous waste sites and ground water pollution," *Archives of Environmental Health*, 44, 2: 69–74.

Grimes, P. and Kentor, J. (2003) "Exporting the greenhouse: Foreign capital penetration and CO_2 emissions 1980–1996," *Journal of World-Systems Research*, 9, 2: 261–75.

Grossman, A. and Rangan, V.K. (2000) *Managing Multi-site Nonprofits*. Harvard Business School Social Enterprise Series, Number 8. Online. Available at <www.hbs.edu/socialenterprise/pdf/SE8ManagingMultiSite Nonprofits.pdf> (accessed 4 July 2012).

Groves, M.J. (1994) "Are smelly animals happy animals? Competing definitions of laboratory animal cruelty and public policy," *Society and Animals*, 2, 2: 125–44.

Groves, M.J. (1996) *Hearts and Minds: The Controversy Over Laboratory Animals*. Temple, PA: Temple University Press.

Gunningham, N.A., Thornton, D. and Kagan, R.A. (2005) "Motivating management: Corporate compliance in environmental protection," *Law and Policy*, 27, 2: 289–316.

Hagan, J. (1994) *Crime and Disrepute*. Thousand Oaks, CA: Pine Forge.

Hall, D. (2002) "Environmental change, protest, and havens of environmental degradation: Evidence from Asia," *Global Environmental Politics*, 2, 2: 20–8.

Hammersley, G. (1973) "The charcoal iron industry and its fuel, 1540–1750," *Economic History Review*, 26, 4: 593–619.

Hart, I.B. (2006) *James Watt and the History of Steam Power*. Montana: Kessinger Publishing.

Havercamp, S.J. (1998) "Are moderate animal welfare laws and a sustainable agricultural economy mutually exclusive? Laws, moral implications, and recommendations," *Drake Law Review*, 645: 645–6.

Herzog, H. (1993) "Human morality and animal research: Confessions and quandaries," *American Scholar*, 62, 3: 337–49.

HFA (Humane Farming Association) (2012) *HFA Campaign Against Factory Farming Subject of HBO Documentary*. Online. Available at < http://hfa. org> (accessed 16 January 2013).

Hillyard, P. and Tombs, S. (2007) "From crime to social harm?" *Crime, Law and Social Change*, 48, 1: 9–25.

Hillyard, P., Pantazis, C., Tombs, S. and Gordon, D. (2004) *Beyond Criminology: Taking Harm Seriously*. London: Pluto.

Homer-Dixon, T.F. (1991) "Environmental changes as causes of acute conflict," *International Security*, 16, 2: 76–116.

Hooks, G. and Smith, C.L. (2005) "Treadmills of production and destruction: Threats to the environment posed by militarization," *Organization and Environment*, 18, 1: 19–37.

Houghton, J.T., Meiro-Filho, L.G., Callander, B.A., Harris, N., Kattenburg, A. and Maskell, K. (1996) *Climate Change 1995: The Science of Climate Change*. Contribution of Working Group I to the Second Assessment Report of the Intergovernmental Panel on Climate Change (Vol. 19390). Cambridge: Cambridge University Press.

Hribal, J. (2003) "Animals are part of the working class: A challenge to labor history," *Labor History*, 44, 4: 435–53.

Humborg, C., Conley, D.J., Rahm, L., Wulff, A.C. and Ittekkot, V. (2000) "Silicon retention in river basins: Far-reaching effects on biogeochemistry and aquatic food webs in coastal marine environments," *Ambio*, 29: 45–50.

Huss, S., Stretesky, P.B. and Lynch M.J. (2012) "Characteristics of the formalized environmental justice movement: Implications for environmental governance," in D. Gallagher (ed.) *Environmental Leadership: A Reference Handbook*. Thousand Oaks, CA: Sage.

International Energy Agency (2012). *Key World Energy Statistics* Online. Available at <www.iea.org/publications/freepublications/publication/kwes.pdf> (accessed 6 November 2012).

International Rivers (2012) *Questions and Answers about Large Dams*. Online. Available at <www.internationalrivers.org/questions-and-answers-about-large-dams> (accessed 20 March 2013).

IPCC (2007) *Impacts, Adaptation and Vulnerability*. Contribution of Working Group II to the Fourth Assessment Report of the Intergovernmental Panel on Climate Change. Cambridge: Cambridge University Press.

Jacobson, J. (1988) *Environmental Refugees: A Yardstick of Habitability*. Worldwatch Paper 86. Washington, DC: Worldwatch Institute.

Jarrell, M.L. (2010) *Environmental Crime and the Media: News Coverage of Petroleum Refining Industry Violations*. NY: LFB Scholarly.

Jarrell, M.L., and Ozymy, J. (2010) "Excessive air pollution and the oil industry: Fighting for our rights to breathe clean air," *Environmental Justice*, 3, 3: 111–15.

Johnson, E.A. and Miyanishi, K. (2008) "Creating new landscapes and ecosystems: The Alberta oil sands," *The Year in Ecology and Conservation Biology 2008*: 120–45.

Jorgenson, A.K. (2011) "Carbon dioxide emissions in Central and Eastern European nations, 1992–2005: A test of ecologically unequal exchange theory," *Human Ecology Review*, 18, 2: 105.

Jorgenson, A.K. and Clark, B. (2011) "Societies consuming nature: A panel study of the ecological footprints of nations, 1960–2003," *Social Science Research*, 40, 1: 226–44.

Kahl, C.H. (1998) "Population growth, environmental degradation, and state-sponsored violence: The case of Kenya, 1991–93," *International Security*, 23, 2: 80–119.

Karliner, J. (1998) *The Corporate Planet*. San Francisco: Sierra Book Club.

Keating, M., Baum, E. and Round, M. (2000) *Laid to Waste: The Dirty Secret of Combustion Waste from America's Power Plants*. Denver, CO: Citizens Coal Council. Online. Available at <www.precaution.org/lib/laid_to_ waste.000601.pdf> (accessed 6 November 2012).

Kennedy, D.M. (2012) *Deterrence and Crime Prevention: Reconsidering the Prospect of Sanction*. London: Routledge.

Kerr, R. (2012) "Learning how to not make your own earthquake," *Science*, 335, 6075: 1436–7.

Khan, S., Cao, Q., Zheng, Y.M., Huang, Y.Z. and Zhu, Y.G. (2008) "Health risks of heavy metals in contaminated soils and food crops irrigated with wastewater in Beijing, China," *Environmental Pollution*, 152, 3: 686–92.

Kim, E.Y., Ichihashi, H., Saeki, K., Atrashkevich, G., Tanabe, S. and Tatsukawa, R. (1996) "Metal accumulation in tissues of seabirds from Chaun, northeast Siberia, Russia," *Environmental Pollution*, 92, 3: 247–52.

Kirilenko, A. and Sedjo, R.A. (2007) "Climate change impacts forestry," *Proceedings of the National Academy of Sciences of the United States*, 104, 50: 19697–702.

Knight, O. and Stretesky, P. B. (2011) "What drives the location of environmental enforcement non-governmental organizations? A look at multinational non-governmental organizations, 1990–2008," paper presented at the Annual Conference of the European Society of Criminology, Vilnius, Lithuania (20 September).

Koh, L.P. and Wilcove, D.S. (2008) "Is oil palm agriculture really destroying tropical biodiversity?" *Conservation Letters*, 1, 2: 60–4.

Kraft, M.E. and Vig, N.J. (2000) *Environmental Policy: New Directions for the Twenty First Century,* Washington, DC: CQ Press.

Krajick, K. (2005) "Fire in the hole," *Smithsonian Magazine*. Online. Available at <www.smithsonianmag.com/travel/firehole.html> (accessed 4 November 2012).

Kramer, R.C. (2012) "Carbon in the atmosphere and power in America: Climate change as state-corporate crime," *Journal of Crime and Justice*. DOI:10.1080/0735648X.2012.752252.

Kramer, R.C. and Michalowski, R. (2012) "Is global warming a state-corporate crime?" in R. White (ed.) *Climate Change from a Criminological Perspective*. New York: Springer.

Kramer, R.C., Michalowski, R.J. and Kauzlarich, D. (2002) "The origins and development of the concept and theory of state-corporate crime," *Crime and Delinquency*, 48: 263–82.

Kubrin, C.E. and Weitzer, R. (2003) "New directions in social disorganization theory," *Journal of Research in Crime in Delinquency*, 40, 4: 374–402.

Kuenzer, C., Zhang, J., Tetzlaff, A., Van Dijk, P., Voigt, S., Mehl, H. and Wagner, W. (2007) "Uncontrolled coalfires and their environmental impacts: Investigating two arid mining regions in north-central China," *Applied Geography*, 27, 1: 42–62.

Lanier-Graham, S.D. (1993) *The Ecology of War: Environmental Impacts of Weaponry and Warfare*. New York: Walker.

Lavelle, M. (2009) *The Clean Coal Lobbying Blitz*. Center for Public Integrity. Online. Available at <www.publicintegrity.org/articles/entry/1284/> (accessed 5 November 2012).

Lazrus, H. (2010) "Water scarcity and climate change in Tuvalu," *Anthropology News*, 51: 25.

Leeming, F.C., Dwyer, W.O. and Bracken, B.A. (1995) "Children's environmental attitude and knowledge scale: Construction and validation," *Journal of Environmental Education*, 26, 3: 22–31.

Lemieux, A.M. and Clarke, R.V. (2009) "The international ban on ivory sales and its effects on elephant poaching in Africa," *British Journal of Criminology*, 49, 4: 451–71.

Liebsch, D., Marques, C.M. and Goldenberg, R. (2008) "How long does the Atlantic rain forest take to recover after an ecological disturbance?" *Biological Conservation*, 141, 6: 1717–25.

Linley, D. (2012) *Fracking under Pressure: The Environmental and Social Impacts and Risks of Shale Gas Development*. Online. Available at <http://sustaina-lytics.com/sites/default/files/unconventional-fossil-fuel-shalegas_final.pdf> (accessed 5 November 2012).

Lonergan, S. (1998) "The role of environmental degradation in population displacement," *Environmental Change and Security Project Report*, 4: 5–15.

Long, M.A., Stretesky, P.B., Lynch, M.J. and Fenwick, E. (2012) "Crime in the coal industry: Implications for green criminology and ToP," *Organization and Environment*, 25, 3: 328–46.

Lovelock, J. (2007) *The Revenge of Gaia: Earth's Climate Crisis and the Fate of Humanity*. NY: Basic Books.

Lovelock, J. and Margulis, L. (1974) "Atmospheric homeostasis by and for the biosphere: The Gaia hypothesis," *Tellus*, 26, 1–2: 2–10.

Lynch, M.J. (1990) "The greening of criminology: A perspective for the 1990s," *Critical Criminologist*, 2, 3: 3–4, 11–12; reprinted in P. Beirne and N. South (eds) (2007) *Green Criminology*. Aldershot: Ashgate.

Lynch, M.J. and Michalowski, R.J. (2006) *A Primer in Radical Criminology*. Monsey, NY: Criminal Justice Press.

Lynch, M.J. and Stretesky, P.B. (2001) "Toxic crimes: Examining corporate victimization of the general public employing medical and epidemiological evidence," *Critical Criminology*, 10, 3: 153–72.

Lynch, M.J. and Stretesky, P.B. (2003) "The meaning of green: Towards a clarification of the term green and its meaning for the development of a green criminology," *Theoretical Criminology*, 7, 2: 217–38.

Lynch, M.J. and Stretesky, P.B. (2010) "The distribution of water-monitoring organizations across states: Implications for community environmental policing and social justice," paper presented at the annual meeting of the American Society of Criminology, San Francisco, CA (November).

Lynch, M.J. and Stretesky, P.B. (2011a) "Similarities between green criminology and green science: Toward a typology of green criminology," *International Journal of Comparative and Applied Criminal Justice*, 35, 4: 293–306.

Lynch, M.J. and Stretesky, P.B. (2011b) "Toxic crimes," in P. Wilcox and F. Cullen (eds) *Oxford Handbook of Criminology*. New York: Oxford University Press.

Lynch, M.J. and Stretesky, P.B. (2012) "Native Americans, social and environmental justice: Implications for criminology," *Social Justice*, 38, 3: 34–54.

Lynch, M.J. and Stretesky, P.B. (2013) "The distribution of water-monitoring organizations across states: Implications for community environmental policing and social justice," *Policing: An International Journal of Police Strategies and Management*, 36, 1: 6–26.

Lynch, M.J., Nalla, M.K. and Miller, K. (1989) "Cross-cultural perceptions of deviance: The case of Bhopal," *Journal of Research in Crime and Delinquency*, 26: 7–35.

Lynch, M.J., Stretesky, P.B. and Burns, R.G. (2004a) "Determinants of environmental law violation fines against petroleum refineries: Race, ethnicity, income, and aggregation effects," *Society and Natural Resources*, 17, 4: 343–57.

Lynch, M.J., Stretesky, P.B. and Burns, R.G. (2004b) "Slippery business: Race, class and legal determinants of penalties against petroleum refineries," *Journal of Black Studies*, 34, 3: 421–40.

Lynch, M.J., Burns, R.G. and Stretesky, P.B. (2010) "Global warming and state-corporate crime: The politicalization of global warming under the Bush administration," *Crime, Law and Social Change*, 54, 3: 213–39.

Machado, K. (2003) "Unfit for human consumption: Why American beef is making us sick," *Albany Law Review*, 13: 807–9.

McPeak, M. (2001) "Tackling fragmentation and building unity in an international nongovernmental organization," *Nonprofit Management and Leadership*, 11, 4: 477–91.

Magdoff, F. and Foster, J.B. (2011) *What Every Environmentalist Needs to Know about Capitalism*. New York: Monthly Review Press.

Mallon, R. (2005) "The deplorable standard of living faced by farmed animals in America's meat industry and how to improve conditions by eliminating the corporate farm," *Student Scholarship*, paper 66.

Marino, E. (2011) "The long history of environmental migration: Assessing vulnerability construction and obstacles to successful relocation in Shishmaref, Alaska," *Global Environmental Change*, 22, 2: 374–81.

Markowitz, G. and Rosner, D. (2003) *Deceit and Denial: The Deadly Politics of Industrial Pollution*, Vol. 6. Los Angeles: UC Press.

Marx, K. (1842) "Debates on the law of thefts of wood," *Rheinische Zeitung*, 298 (October 25), 300 (October 27), 303 (October 30), 305 (November 1) and 307 (November 3). Online. Available at <www.marxists.org/archive/marx/works/1842/10/25.htm> (accessed 16 January 2013).

Marx, K. (1976 [1867]) *Capital, Vol. I*. Moscow: International Publishers.

Maugeri, L. (2006) *The Age of Oil: The Mythology, History, and Future of the World's Most Controversial Resource*. Westport, CT: Praeger.

Meehl, G.A., Washington, W.M., Collins, W.D., Arblaster, J.M., Hu, A., Buja, L.E., Strand, W.G. and Teng, H. (2005) "How much more global warming and sea level rise?" *Science*, 307, 5716: 1769–72.

Meng, L., Feng, Q., Zhou, L., Lu, P. and Meng Q. (2009) "Environmental cumulative effects of coal underground mining," *Procedia Earth and Planetary Science*, 1, 1: 1280–4.

Merem, E., Robinson, B., Wesley, J.M., Yerramilli, S. and Twumasi, Y.A. (2010) "Using GIS in ecological management: Green assessment of the impacts of petroleum activities in the state of Texas," *International Journal of Environmental Research and Public Health*, 7, 5: 2101–30.

Messner, S.F. and Rosenfeld, R. (2006) *Crime and the American Dream*. Belmont, CA: Wadsworth.

Michalowski, R. and Kramer, R. (2007) "State-corporate crime and criminological inquiry," in H.N. Pontell and G.L. Geis (eds) *International Handbook of White-Collar and Corporate Crime*. New York: Springer.

Mielke, H.W. and Zahran, S. (2012) "The urban rise and fall of air lead (Pb) and the latent surge and retreat of societal violence," *Environment International*, 43: 48–55.

Mikler, J. (2009) *The Greening of the Car Industry*. Northampton, MA: Edward Elgar.

Mills, C.W. (1959) *The Sociological Imagination*. New York, NY: Oxford.

Milovanovic, D. (2006) "Legalistic definition of crime and an alternative view," *Annals of the Faculty of Law in Belgrade – Belgrade Law Review (International Edition)*, 1, 78–86.

Mokhov, A.V. (2011) "Mine water drainage from flooded coal mines," *Doklady Earth Sciences*, 438, 2: 733–5.

Mol, A. (1995) *The Refinement of Production: Ecological Modernization Theory and the Dutch Chemical Industry*. Utrecht: Jan van Arkel/International Books.

Mol, A. and Spaargaren, G. (2000) "Ecological modernization theory in debate: A review," in A. Mol and D. Sonnenfeld (eds) *Ecological Modernization Around the World*. London: Frank Cass.

Molnár, P.K., Derocher, A.E., Thiemann, G.W. and Lewis, M.A. (2010) "Predicting survival, reproduction and abundance of polar bears under climate change," *Biological Conservation*, 143, 7: 1612–22.

Montague, P. (1996) "The pesticide failure," *Rachel's Environment and Health Weekly*, 482. Online. Available at <www.envirolink.org/pubs/rachel> (accessed 16 January 2013).

Montgomery, C.T. and Smith, M.B. (2010) "Hydraulic fracturing: History of an enduring technology," *Journal of Petroleum Technology*, 62: 26–32.

Morales, O., Grineski, S.E. and Collins, T.W. (2012) "Structural violence and environmental injustice: The case of a US–Mexico border chemical plant," *Local Environment*, 17, 1: 1–21.

Mosel, A. (2001) "What about Wilbur? Proposing a federal statute to provide minimum humane living conditions for farm animals raised for food production," *Dayton Law Review*, 27: 133–50.

Müller, B., Berg, M., Yao, Z.P., Zhang, X.F., Wang, D. and Pfluger, A. (2008) "How polluted is the Yangtze river? Water quality downstream from the Three Gorges Dam," *Science of the Total Environment*, 402, 2: 232–47.

Myers, B., Thomas, R. and McElfish, J. (2007) *Clean Water Act Jurisdictional Handbook*. Washington, DC: Environmental Law Institute.

Myers, N. (1993) "Environmental refugees in a globally warmed world," *Bioscience*, 43, 11: 752–61.

Myrup, M. (2012) "Industrialising Greenland: Government and transnational corporations versus civil society?" in R. Ellefsen, R. Sollund and G. Larsen (eds) *Eco-global Crimes: Contemporary Problems and Future Challenges*. London: Ashgate.

Narag, R.E., Pizarro, J. and Gibbs, C. (2009) "Lead exposure and its implications for criminological theory," *Criminal Justice and Behavior*, 36, 9: 954–73.

Nature Conservancy (2011) *Forest Conservation: Responsible Trade Combating Illegal Logging and Advancing Responsible Forest Trade*. Online. Available at <www.nature.org/ourinitiatives/habitats/forests/howwework/combating-illegal-logging-and-advancing-responsible-forest-trade.xml> (accessed 16 January 2013).

Naughton-Treves, L., Kammen, D.M. and Chapman, C. (2007) "Burning biodiversity: Woody biomass use by commercial and subsistence groups in western Uganda's forests," *Biological Conservation*, 134, 2: 232–41.

Needleman, H. (2009) "Low level lead exposure: History and discovery," *Annals of Epidemiology*, 19, 4: 235–8.

Nieto, J.M., Sarmiento, A.M., Olías, M., Canovas, C.R., Riba, I., Kalman, J. and Delvalls, A. (2007) "Acid mine drainage pollution in the Tinto and Odiel rivers (Iberian Pyrite Belt, SW Spain) and bioavailability of the transported metals to the Huelva Estuary," *Environment International*, 33, 4: 445–55.

Nriagu, J.O. (1990) "Global metal pollution, poisoning the biosphere?" *Environment*, 32, 7: 7–33.

Nurse, A. (2013) *Animal Harm: Perspectives on Why People Harm and Kill Animals*. London: Ashgate.

Obach, B.K. (2004) "New labor: Slowing the ToP?" *Organization and Environment*, 17, 3: 337–54.

O'Connor, J. (1973) *The Fiscal Crisis of the State*. New York: St Martin's Press.

O'Connor, J. (1998) *Natural Causes: Essays in Ecological Marxism*. New York: Guilford Press.

Odum, E. and Barrett, G.W. (2004) *Fundamentals of Ecology*. Belmont, CA: Wadsworth.

Oliver, W. (1998) *Community Oriented Policing: A Systematic Approach to Policing*. New Jersey: Prentice-Hall.

Opukri, C.O. and Ibaba, I.S. (2008) "Oil induced environmental degradation and internal population displacement in Nigeria's Niger Delta," *Journal of Sustainable Development in Africa*, 10, 1: 173–93.

O'Rourke, D. and Macey, G. (2003) "Community environmental policing: Assessing new strategies for public participation in environmental regulation," *Journal of Policy Analysis and Management*, 22: 383–14.

Orsato, R.J., den Hond, F. and Clegg, S.R. (2002) "The political ecology of automobile recycling in Europe," *Organization Studies*, 23, 4: 639–65.

Osborne, S.J., Shy, C.M. and Kaplan, B.M. (1990) "Epidemiologic analysis of a reported cancer cluster in a small rural population," *American Journal of Epidemiology*, 132(1): S87–S95.

Ottinger, G. (2010) "Constructing empowerment through interpretations of environmental data," *Surveillance and Society*, 8: 221–34.

Overdevest, C. and Mayer, B. (2008) "Harnessing the power of information through community monitoring: Insights from social science," *Texas Law Review*, 86: 1494–526.

Pal, M., and Dutta, M.J. (2012) "Organizing resistance on the internet: The case of the international campaign for justice in Bhopal," *Communication, Culture and Critique*, 5, 2: 230–51.

Park, R.E. and Burgess, E.W. (1984 [1919]) *The City*. Chicago, IL: University of Chicago Press.

Parker, L. (2007) "Mining battle marked by peaks and valleys," *USA Today*. Online. Available at <www.usatoday.com/news/nation/2007-04-18-mines_N.htm> (accessed 13 October 2008).

Parker, R. (1995) "Coal mining mutiny," *Albuquerque Journal*, January 22: A1.

Pearce, F. and Tombs, S. (1998) *Toxic Capitalism: Corporate Crime and the Chemical Industry*. Brookfield, VT: Ashgate.

Pellow, D.N. (2000) "Environmental inequality formation: Toward a theory of environmental injustice," *American Behavioral Scientist*, 43, 4: 581–601.

Pires, S.F., and Clarke, R.V. (2011) "Sequential foraging, itinerant fences and parrot poaching in Bolivia," *British Journal of Criminology*, 51, 2: 314–35.

Pires, S.F., and Clarke, R.V. (2012) "Are parrots CRAVED? An analysis of parrot poaching in Mexico," *Journal of Research in Crime and Delinquency*, 49, 1: 122–46.

Pond, G., Passmore, M., Borsuk, F., Reynolds, L. and Rose, C. (2008) "Downstream effects of mountaintop coal mining: Comparing biological conditions using family- and genus-level macroinvertebrate bioassessment tools," *Journal of the North American Benthological Society*, 27: 717–37.

Porter, G. (1999) "Trade competition and pollution standards: 'Race to the bottom' or 'stuck at the bottom'," *Journal of Environment and Development*, 8, 2: 133–51.

Post, J.E. (2012) "The United Nations Global Compact: A CSR milestone," *Business and Society*, DOI: 10.1177/0007650312459926.

Pujades-Rodríguez, M., McKeever, T., Lewis, S., Whyatt, D., Britton, J. and Venn, A. (2009) "Effect of traffic pollution on respiratory and allergic disease in adults: Cross-sectional and longitudinal analyses," *BMC Pulmonary Medicine*, 9, 1: 42–52.

Quinney, R. (2008 [1970]) *The Social Construction of Crime*. Brunswick: NJ: Transaction.

Quinney, R. (1980) *Class, State, and Crime*. New York: Longman.

Ramanathan, V. and Feng, Y. (2009) "Air pollution, greenhouse gases and climate change: Global and regional perspectives," *Atmospheric Environment*, 43, 1: 37–50.

Raphael, S. and Winter-Ebmer, R. (2001) "Identifying the effect of unemployment on crime," *Journal of Law and Economics*, 44: 259–83.

Ray, J. and S. Jones (2011) "Self-reported psychopathic traits and their relation to intentions to engage in environmental offending," *International Journal of Offender Therapy and Comparative Criminology*, 55, 3: 370–91.

Reece, E. (2006) *Lost Mountain: A Year in the Vanishing Wilderness*. New York: Riverhead Books.

Reed, G.E. and Yeager, P.C. (1996) "Organizational offending and neoclassical criminology: Challenging the reach of a general theory of crime," *Criminology*, 34, 2: 357–82.

Reiman, J. (2007) *The Rich Get Richer and the Poor Get Prison*. Boston, MA: Allyn and Bacon.

Reopanichkul, P., Carter, R.W., Worachananant, S. and Crossland, C.J. (2010) "Wastewater discharge degrades coastal waters and reef communities in southern Thailand," *Marine Environmental Research*, 69, 5: 287–96.

Reuters (2012) *June US Auto Sales in Line with 2012 Estimates*. Online. Available at <http://in.reuters.com/article/2012/07/06/idINWNA0516201120/06> (accessed 29 July 2012).

Reynolds, C.S. (2006) *Ecology of Phytoplankton*. MA: Cambridge University Press.

Rhodes, E.L. (2005) *Environmental Justice in America: A New Paradigm*. Bloomington, IN: Indiana University Press.

Rhodes, W.M., Allen, E.P. and Callahan, M. (2006) *Illegal Logging: A Market-based Analysis of Trafficking in Illegal Timber*. ABT Associates. Online. Available at <www.ncjrs.gov/pdffiles1/nij/grants/215344.pdf> (accessed 4 November 2012).

Rifkin, J. (1995) *The End of Work: The Decline of the Global Labor Force and the Dawn of the Post-Market Era*. New York: Putnam.

Rios, J.M. (2000) "Environmental justice groups: Grass-roots movement or NGO networks? Some policy implications," *Policy Studies Review*, 17: 179–211.

Robertson, S.J., McGill, W.B., Massicotte, H.B. and Rutherford, P.M. (2007) "Petroleum hydrocarbon contamination in boreal forest soils: A mycorrhizal ecosystems perspective," *Biological Reviews*, 82, 2: 213–40.

Rosner, D. and Markowitz, G. (2007) "The politics of lead toxicology and the devastating consequences for children," *American Journal of Industrial Medicine*, 50, 10: 740–56.

Ross, M.L. (1999) "The political economy of the resource curse," *World Politics*, 51: 297–322.

Ryan, W. (1981) *Equality*. New York: Vintage.

Salo, R.S. (2004) "When the logs roll over: The need for an international convention criminalizing involvement in the global illegal timber," *Georgetown International Environmental Law Review*, 16: 127–48.

Sampson, R.J. and Groves, W.B. (1989) "Community structure and crime: Testing social-disorganization theory," *American Journal of Sociology*, 94, 4: 774–802.

Savitz, A.W. (2006) *The Triple Bottom Line: How Today's Best-run Companies Are Achieving Economic, Social and Environmental Success – And How You Can Too*. San Francisco, CA: Jossey-Bass.

Schallenberg, R. (1975) "Evolution, adaptation and survival: The very slow death of the American charcoal iron industry," *Annals of Science*, 32, 4: 341–58.

Schelly, D. and Stretesky, P.B. (2009) "An analysis of the 'path of least resistance' argument in three environmental justice success cases," *Society and Natural Resources*, 22, 4: 369–80.

Schnaiberg, A. (1980) *The Environment: From Surplus to Scarcity*. New York: Oxford University Press.

Schnaiberg, A. and Gould, K.A. (1994) *Environment and Society: The Enduring Conflict*. New York: St Martin's Press.

Schnaiberg, A., Pellow, D.N. and Weinberg, A. (2002) "The treadmill of production and the environmental state," in A. Mol and F. Buttel (eds) *The Environmental State Under Pressure*. London: Elsevier.

Schorn, D. (2005) "Burning rage," *60 Minutes*. Online. Available at <www.cbsnews.com/2100-18560_162-1036067.html> (accessed 4 July 2012).

Schroeder, D.V. (2000) *Introduction to Thermal Physics*. New York: Addison Wesley Longman.

Schutz, H., Moll, S. and Bringezu, S. (2004) *Globalisation and the Shifting Environmental Burden*. Online. Available at <www.wupperinst.org/uploads/tx_wibeitrag/WP134e.pdf> (accessed 10 August 2012).

Schwaner, S.L. and Keil, T.J. (2003) "Internal colonization, folk justice, and murder in Appalachia: The case of Kentucky," *Journal of Criminal Justice*, 31, 3: 279–86.

Sebbenn, A.M., Degen, B., Azevedo, V.C., Silva, M.B., de Lacerda, A.E., Ciampi, A.Y., Kanashiro, M., Carneiro, F., Thompson, I. and Loveless, M.D. (2008) "Modeling the long-term impacts of selective logging on genetic diversity and demographic structure of four tropical tree species in the Amazon forest," *Forest Ecology and Management*, 245, 2: 335–49.

Shahabpour, J., Doorandish, M. and Abbasnejad, A. (2005) "Mine-drainage water from coal mines of Kerman region, Iran," *Environmental Geology*, 47: 915–25.

Shaw, C.R. and McKay, H.D. (1942) *Juvenile Delinquency and Urban Areas*. Chicago, IL: University of Chicago Press.

Shelley, T.O.C., Chiricos, T. and Gertz, M. (2011) "What about the environment? Assessing the perceived seriousness of environmental crime," *International Journal of Comparative and Applied Criminal Justice*, 35, 4: 307–325.

Shoko, D.S. (2002) "Small-scale mining and alluvial gold panning within the Zambezi Basin: An ecological time bomb and tinderbox for future conflicts among riparian states," paper presented at the ninth conference of the International Association for the Study of Common Property, *The Commons in an Age of Globalization*, Victoria Falls, Zimbabwe (June 17–21).

Shover, N., Clelland, D. and Lynxwiler, J. (1986) *Enforcement or Negotiation: The Construction of a Regulatory Bureaucracy*. Albany: State University of New York Press.

Simon, D.R. (2000) "Corporate environmental crimes and social inequality: New directions for environmental justice research," *American Behavioral Scientist*, 43, 4: 633–45.

Sindermann, C.J. (1979) "Pollution-associated diseases and abnormalities of fish and shellfish: A review," *Fish Bulletin*, 76, 4: 717–49.

Situ, Y. (1997) "A pathway to the knowledge of environmental crime: Learning through service," *Journal of Criminal Justice Education*, 8, 2: 243–51.

Skogan, W.G. and Harnett, S.M. (1997) *Community Policing, Chicago Style*. Oxford: Oxford University Press.

Smith, J. and Wiest, D. (2005) "The uneven geography of global civil society: National and global influences on transnational association," *Social Forces*, 84, 2: 621–52.

Smith, M. and Voreacos, D. (2007) "Brazil: Enslaved workers make charcoal used to make basic steel ingredient," *Seattle Times*, 21 January.

Smith, W.B., Miles, P.D., Perry, C.H. and Pugh, S.A. (2009) *Forest Resources of the United States, 2007*. General Technical Report WO-78. Washington, DC: United States Department of Agriculture, Forest Service.

Sollund, R. (2011) "Expressions of speciesism: The effects of keeping companion animals on animal abuse, animal trafficking and species decline," *Crime, Law and Social Change*, 55, 5: 437–51.

Somerville, P. (2009) "Understanding community policing," *Policing: An International Journal of Police Strategies and Management*, 32: 261–77.

South, N. and Brisman, A. (eds) (2012) *Routledge International Handbook of Green Criminology*. New York: Routledge.

Spitzer, S. (1975) "Toward a Marxian theory of deviance," *Social Problems*, 22, 5: 638–51.

Srivastava, L., Schwartz, S.L. and Austin, M.J. (2012) *Managing Non-governmental Organizations Worldwide: Mapping the Knowledge Base of Nonprofit Management in the Human Services*. Online. Available at <www.mackcenter.org/docs/NGOs%20Worldwide.pdf> (accessed 4 July 2012).

Stanford, C.B. (2010) *The Last Tortoise: A Tale of Extinction in our Lifetime*. Cambridge, MA: Harvard University Press.

Stauber, J.C. and Rampton, R. (1995) *Toxic Sludge is Good For You!* Monroe, ME: Common Courage Press.

Stickler, C. (2012) *A Deadly Way of Doing Business: A Case Study of Corporate Crime in the Coal Mining Industry*. Master's thesis, Department of Criminology, University of South Florida.

Stracher, G. and Taylor, T. (2004) "Coal fires burning out of control around the world: Thermodynamic recipe for environmental catastrophe," *International Journal of Coal Geology*, 59: 7–17.

Stretesky, P.B. (2006) "Corporate self-policing and the environment," *Criminology*, 44, 3: 671–708.

Stretesky, P.B. (2008) "The neglect of race and class in environmental crime research," in M.J. Lynch and R. Paternoster (eds) *Racial and Ethnic Bias in the Criminal Justice System*. New York, NY: Criminal Justice Press.

Stretesky, P.B. and Lynch, M.J. (1999a) "Environmental justice and prediction of distance to accidental chemical releases in Hillsborough County, Florida," *Social Science Quarterly*, 80, 4: 830–46.

Stretesky, P.B. and Lynch, M.J. (1999b) "Corporate environmental violence and racism," *Crime, Law and Social Change*, 30, 2: 163–84.

Stretesky, P.B. and Lynch, M.J. (2001) "The relationship between lead exposure and homicide," *Archives of Pediatrics and Adolescent Medicine*, 155, 5: 579–89.

Stretesky, P.B. and Lynch, M.J. (2002) "Environmental hazards and school segregation in Hillsborough County Florida, 1987–1999," *Sociological Quarterly*, 43, 4: 553–73.

Stretesky, P.B. and Lynch, M.J. (2004) "The relationship between lead and crime," *Journal of Health and Social Behavior*, 45, 2: 214–29.

Stretesky, P.B. and Lynch, M.J. (2009) "A cross-national study of the association between per capita carbon dioxide emissions and exports to the United States," *Social Science Research*, 38, 1: 239–50.

Stretesky, P.B. and Lynch, M.J. (2011) "Coal strip mining, mountaintop removal, and the distribution of environmental violations across the United States, 2002–2008," *Landscape Research*, 36, 2: 209–30.

Stretesky, P.B., Shelley, T.O. and Crow, M.S. (2010) "Do conservation organizations influence the social production of natural resource violations?" *Organization and Environment*, 23, 4: 398–16.

Stretesky, P.B., Huss, S., Lynch, M.J., Zahran, S. and Childs, B. (2011) "The founding of environmental justice organizations across US counties during the 1990s and 2000s: Civil rights and environmental cross-movement effects," *Social Problems*, 58: 330–60.

Stretesky, P.B., Long, M.A. and Lynch, M.J. (2012) "Does environmental enforcement slow the ToP?" *Journal of Crime and Justice*. DOI: 10.1080/0735648X.2012.752254.

Strohm, L.A. (2002) "Pollution havens and the transfer of environmental risk," *Global Environmental Politics*, 2, 2: 29–36.

Sutherland, E.H. (1949) *White Collar Crime*. New York: Dryden Press.

Switzer, J. (2002) "Oil and violence in Sudan," paper prepared for the African Centre for Technology Studies. Online. Available at <www.iisd.org/pdf/2002/envsec_oil_violence.pdf> (accessed 16 January 2013).

Szasz, A. (1986) "Corporations, organized crime, and the disposal of hazardous waste: An examination of the making of a criminogenic regulatory structure," *Criminology*, 24: 1–27.

Tacconi, L. (2007a) *Illegal Logging: Law Enforcement, Livelihoods and the Timber Trade*. London: Earthscan.

Tacconi, L. (2007b) "Deforestation and climate change," in W. Steffen, L. Tacconi and F. Jotzo (eds) *Climate Change and Public Policy*. Canberra: Crawford School of Economics and Government, Australian National University.

Thomas, W.I. and Znaniecki, F. (1919) *The Polish Peasant in Europe and America*. Boston, MA: Gorham Press.

Thornton, D., Gunningham, N.A. and Kagan, R.A. (2005) "General deterrence and corporate environmental behavior," *Law and Policy*, 27, 2: 262–88.

Tiwary, R.K. (2001) "Environmental impact of coal mining on water regime and its management," *Water, Air, and Soil Pollution*, 132: 185–99.

Tombs, S. (2012) "State complicity in the production of corporate crime," in J. Gobert and A. Pascal (eds) *European Developments in Corporate Criminal Liability*. London: Routledge.

Truhaut, R. (1977) "Ecotoxicology: Objectives, principles and perspectives," *Ecotoxicology and Environmental Safety* 1, 2: 151–73.

Tyndall, J. (1861) "On the absorption and radiation of heat by gases and vapours, and on the physical connexion of radiation, absorption, and conduction: The Bakerian Lecture," *London, Edinburgh, and Dublin Philosophical Magazine and Journal of Science*, 22, 146: 169–94.

UNEP (United Nations Environmental Programme) (2012) *Annual Report, 2011*. ISBN: 978-92-807-3244-3. Online. Available at <www.unep.org/annualreport/2011/docs/UNEP_ANNUAL_REPORT_2011.pdf> (accessed 13 February 2012).

US Department of Transportation, Federal Highway Administration, Office of Highway Information (2012) *Traffic Volume Trends*. Online. Available at <www.fhwa.dot.gov/> (accessed 29 July 2012).

US Energy Information Administration (2006) *Coal Production in the United States*. Online. Available at <www.eia.doe.gov/cneaf/coal/page/coal_production_review.pdf> (accessed 10 November 2008).

US Energy Information Administration (2011) *Monthly Energy Review, April 2011*. DOE/EIA-0035(2011/04). Online. Available at <www.eia.gov/totalenergy/data/monthly/archive/00351104.pdf> (accessed 15 March 2013).

US Energy Information Administration (2012a) *Petroleum and Other Liquids*. Online. Available at <www.eia.gov/dnav/pet/hist/LeafHandler.ashx?n=pet&s=mcrfpus2&f=a> (accessed 6 November 2012).

US Energy Information Administration (2012b) *Monthly Energy Review, July 2012*. DOE/EIA-0035(2012/07). Online. Available at <www.eia.gov/totalenergy/data/monthly/pdf/mer.pdf> (accessed 29 July 2012).

US Environmental Protection Agency (2002) *Starting Out in Volunteer Water-monitoring*. EPA 841-F-02-004. Office of Water, United States Environmental Protection Agency, Washington, DC.

US Environmental Protection Agency (2012) *Light-duty Automotive Technology, Carbon Dioxide Emissions, and Fuel Economy Trends: 1975 through 2011*. EPA-420-R-12-001. Online. Available at <www.epa.gov/otaq/cert/mpg/fetrends/2012/420r12001.pdf> (accessed 29 July 2012).

Vail, B.J. (2007) "Illegal waste transport and the Czech Republic: An environmental sociological perspective," *Czech Sociological Review*, 43, 6: 1195–211.

Vanderheiden, S. (2005) "Eco-terrorism or justified resistance? Radical environmentalism and the war on terror," *Politics and Society*, 33: 425–47.

Van der Hoeven, F.D. (2012) "Leidsche Rijn: Balancing the compact city with the Randstad motorway network," in S. Polyzos (ed.) *Urban Development*. InTech.

Van Groenigen, K.J., Osenberg, C.W. and Hungate, B.A. (2011) "Increased soil emissions of potent greenhouse gases under increased atmospheric CO_2," *Nature*, 475, 7355: 214–16.

Veysey, B.M. and Messner, S.F. (1999) "Further testing of social disorganization theory: An elaboration of Sampson and Groves's 'community structure and crime'," *Journal of Research in Crime and Delinquency*, 36, 2: 156–74.

Wackernagel, M. and Rees, W. (1996) *Our Ecological Footprint: Reducing Human Impact on the Earth*. Gabriola Island, Canada: New Society Publishers.

Walker, C.H., Hopkins, S.P., Sibley, R.M. and Peakall, D.B. (2006) *Principles of Ecotoxicology*. Boca Raton, FL: Taylor and Francis.

Walker, G. (2012) "A necessary social understanding of the natural sciences," in M. Clifford and T.D. Edwards (eds) *Environmental Crime*, 2nd edition. Burlington, MA: Jones and Bartlett.

Walker, S. (2006) *Sense and Nonsense about Crime and Drugs*, 6th edition. Belmont, CA: Wadsworth.

Walters, R. (2007) "Politics, economy and environmental crime," *Criminal Justice Matters*, 70, 1: 27–28.

Walters, R. (2010) "Toxic atmospheres: Air pollution, trade and the politics of regulation," *Critical Criminology*, 18, 4: 307–23.

Walther, G.R., Beißner, S. and Burga, C.A. (2009) "Trends in the upward shift of alpine plants," *Journal of Vegetation Science*, 16, 5: 541–48.

Warchol, G.L. and Kapla, D. (2012) "Policing the wilderness: A descriptive study of wildlife conservation officers in South Africa," *International Journal of Comparative and Applied Criminal Justice*, 36, 2: 83–101.

Warchol, G.L., Zuppan, L.L. and Clack, W. (2003) "Transnational criminality: An analysis of the illegal wildlife market in Southern Africa," *International Criminal Justice Review*, 13, 1: 1–27.

Warrick, J. (2001) "They die piece by piece," *Washington Post*, April 11: A01.

Westerhuis, D., Walters, R. and Wyatt, T. (eds) (2013) *Emerging Issues in Green Criminology*. New York: Palgrave Macmillan.

White, R. (2008) *Crimes Against Nature: Environmental Criminology and Ecological Justice*. Cullompton: Willan.

White, R. (2012a) "Risk and environmental victimisation," in B. Thomas and S. Lockie (eds) *Risk and Social Theory in Environmental Management*. Collingwood, Australia: CSIRO.

White, R. (2012b) *Climate Change from a Criminological Perspective*. New York, NY: Springer.

White, R. and Heckenberg, D. (2011) "Environmental horizon scanning and criminological researcher and practice," *European Journal of Criminal Policy and Research*, 17, 2: 87–100.

Wilcove, D.S. and Wikelski, M. (2008) "Going, going, gone. Is animal migration disappearing," *PLoS Biology*, 6, 7: e188.

Wolfe, A. (1977) *The Limits of Legitimacy: Political Contradictions of Contemporary Capitalism*. New York: Free Press.

Woods, N.D. (2006) "Interstate competition and environmental regulation: A test of the race to the bottom thesis," *Social Science Quarterly*, 87, 1: 174–89.

Wright, T. (2004) "The political economy of coal mine disasters in China: 'Your rice bowl or your life'," *China Quarterly*, 179: 629–46.

Wyatt, T. (2013) "From the Cardamom Mountains of Southwest Cambodia to the forests of the world: An exploration of the illegal charcoal trade," *International Journal of Comparative and Applied Criminal Justice*, 37, 1: 15–29.

Xu, J., Grumbine, R.E., Shrestha, A., Eriksson, M., Yang, X., Wang, Y. and Wilkes, A. (2009) "The melting Himalayas: Cascading effects of climate change on water, biodiversity, and livelihoods," *Conservation Biology*, 23, 3: 520–30.

Yale Law School (2011) *Environmental Law*. Career Development Office. Online. Available at <www.law.yale.edu/Body_2011_PUBLIC.pdf> (accessed 4 July 2012).

Yardley, J. (2004) "Rivers run black, and Chinese die of cancer," *New York Times*, 12 September. Online. Available at <www.nytimes.com/2004/09/12/international/asia/12china.html?pagewanted=print&p&_r=0> (accessed 6 January 2013).

Ydersbond, I.M. (2012) *Multi-level lobbying in the EU: The Case of the Renewables Directive and the German Energy Industry*. Masters thesis, University of Oslo, Norway. Online. Available at <www.duo.uio.no/bitstream/handle/123456789/13181/ydersbond.pdf?sequence=3> (accessed 16 January 2013).

Yeager, P.C. (1993) *The Limits of Law: The Public Regulation of Private Pollution*. Cambridge: Cambridge University Press.

York, R. (2004) "The treadmill of (diversifying) production," *Organization and Environment*, 17, 3: 355–62.

Yusoff, S. (2003) "Renewable energy from palm oil: Innovation on effective utilization of waste," *Journal of Cleaner Production*, 14: 87–93.

Zakrzewski, S.F. (2002). *Environmental Toxicology*. New York: Oxford University Press.

Zimring, F.E. and Hawkins, G. (1973) *Deterrence: The Legal Threat in Crime Control*. Chicago: University of Chicago Press.

INDEX